Stay in the Buggy

THE STORY OF AN ORDINARY WOMAN DOING EXTRAORDINARY THINGS

GAYLE CRANSTON

THE STORY OF AN ORDINARY WOMAN DOING EXTRAORDINARY THINGS

Dedicated to my family, in memory of my mother Kate.

ISBN: 979 883 91158566

Cover design by rachael@rachaelritchey.com

Editing and interior design by Sallianne Hines (quinneditingservices@gmail.com)

Buggy sketch by Margaret Schmidt (dusemz@venturecomm.net)

Kathryn Wilson Gunderson Larsen

A proud patriot, a pioneer feminist, an ordinary woman
doing extraordinary things.
Kate was my heroine,
and my mother.

You could buy a package of gum or an ice cream cone for 5¢.

When some kids were expected to "get by" with a quarter for spending money while going to high school.

When rural boys and girls stayed in dorms or private homes to go to high school.

When we set hens and hatched baby chicks and the hens—with our help—cared for the babies.

When Mom baked bread every other day for a family of nine kids.

When radio and television weren't, and we created our own entertainment.

When Mom went to the court house in Gann Valley to buy our textbooks (I presume with the recommendation of the county superintendent). Later the school district bought the books, as now.

When the seventh and eighth graders went to the county courthouse to write final exams.

When the compulsory education law was passed which made school attendance compulsory for all boys and girls until age sixteen or until they passed the eighth grade.

When the cream and egg check bought gas and groceries, and Prince Albert tobacco cost only 25¢.

When men rolled their own cigarettes.

When a new Ford roadster cost $825. And we thought that was a fortune.

When we all had a pail of drinking water and a common dipper from which we drank. And we seldom got sick.

When we had to pick cobs after school for fuel for the cooking range.

When the yard got mowed once, or maybe twice a year with the field mower.

When, in the "dirty thirties" dust was everywhere, outdoors in banks and indoors in layers.

When our husbands worked on the WPA (Works Progress Administration).

Memories recorded by Kate

ONE

Charlie Meets Anna

ANNA SICK, mother of Kate Wilson Gunderson Larsen, emigrated to Omaha, Nebraska from Germany early in the year 1900, joining family members who had arrived before her. Her family in America had encouraged Anna to journey there and promised to help her become familiar with the culture and find employment after her arrival.

The Sick family received word that a ranch owner they had contacted about a maid job for Anna was interested in speaking with her. The need was great and he was ready to hire. Her siblings took her to see the ranch, and helped her communicate with the owner about her ability to perform the required duties. She was pleased to find they all felt her adequately prepared to perform the required tasks and she was asked to begin work immediately.

One of the ranch hands there, Charlie Wilson, was a little flirtatious, often smiling and winking at her. They began communicating and became good friends. He offered to help her learn English and soon their friendship became a romance. Charlie and Anna were married in December of 1900.

Following their marriage, they moved to Kansas to live with

Charlie's parents. Charlie worked for the railroad. While there, Charlie and Anna's first child, Henry, was born in 1902. Charlie worked long hours and rarely saw Henry or Anna and grew restless for other kinds of employment. He had ideas about being his own boss and owning his own farm. He heard about land opportunities further north, and a yearning stirred deep inside him to be part of the American dream.

Charlie and Anna Wilson, December 1900

One day at work Charlie got into a conversation with a co-worker from Missouri. During their casual chat Charlie indicated he was looking for other work, and shared his dream of owning his own farm and being his own boss. His new friend owned 40 acres in Missouri that "just happens to be for sale."

Charlie could picture himself owning that farm. Before the

conversation ended, Charlie offered to trade his string of horses for the farmland. "Would that be a fair trade?"

His new friend promised to think it over.

When they spoke again, his friend said, "You know, Charlie, I'd like to make that trade. Let's do it!"

Charlie became the proud owner of a farm located in Blue Springs, Missouri.

He liked living in Missouri. He thought the land far superior to Kansas or Nebraska, and with such good soil and mild weather the crop yield was excellent. Anna, however, had nearly stepped on one of many poisonous snakes populating that area and became so nervous and cautious that she refused to let Henry play outside. Soon Anna was pregnant with their second child. Fred was born in 1904 in Missouri. Charlie wanted to provide a good environment for Anna and the children, and the snake problem seemed insurmountable. He decided they should return to Kansas where Anna was more comfortable.

Charlie was a good carpenter, but those skills didn't seem to be in demand in Kansas so he returned to work at the railroad in Salina. When Anna found she was expecting their third child, they decided it would be best for Anna to be near her siblings in Nebraska during her pregnancy. They moved to Benson, a small suburb of Omaha, and Ira was born there in 1906.

Anna felt good living near her sisters and brothers. She enjoyed their company and it was easy to converse with them in German, her native tongue. But Charlie was left out of their conversations and felt "snubbed" at their family gatherings. He could speak only a few words in German, which Anna had taught him. He had patiently worked with Anna to help her learn English and insisted English would be spoken in his family. He was proud to be an American and he wanted his family to feel that pride.

Relying on his carpentry and masonry skills once again, Charlie began building and repairing homes in Nebraska. Unfortunately, he sustained injuries in a fall from a scaffold. While recuperating, he researched rumors about the Dakotas. He saw ads that promised "lots of sunshine, healthy climate, good fruitful fields, awakening industries and golden opportunities." Wanting to speak to someone knowledgeable about this, he boarded a train to Sioux City, Iowa and went to the Dakota Development Land Company. The agents received him royally and did a good job of describing beautiful land that was "flowing with milk and honey." They spoke about many improvements, such as a small house on the property, a well with good water, and land that was already fenced. Charlie returned home the proud owner of 160 acres of land in Eldorado Township in Buffalo County, South Dakota. The price he paid was $26/acre.

When Charlie broke the news to Anna, he assured her that many other families were settling there. And a train traveled through the nearby town of Kimball so she and the children could return to Omaha to visit her family occasionally.

Preparations were made for two covered wagons to take the family to their new South Dakota home. Charlie acquired four good horses and hired a man to drive one wagon for him. He bought canvas and bows to cover the wagons and carefully customized them himself.

Baby Ira rode in the wagon with Charlie and Anna. Their dog, Bounce, accompanied the family on the journey and happily bounced along with Henry and Fred who held onto a rope while walking or running behind the wagon so they wouldn't wander off. When the boys tired of that, Charlie put them on the seat beside him and told them stories.

At night, the children and Anna slept in the wagon under the protective canvas but Charlie rolled up in blankets underneath the wagon. Each morning, after a filling breakfast, they were on their way again.

As they traveled, the lay of the land changed. There were more hills and the going was slow. The ground was sandy. Perhaps they had reached the Sand Hills of Nebraska. They came to a small town with a large mercantile store and bought more supplies and provisions, then headed for the Missouri River where they would cross over into South Dakota.

At the river there was a strong South Dakota breeze. Charlie observed how the wind and the current had taken the previous ferry-load downstream. He was prepared to double back on the other side of the river. He stood in front of the teams of horses to keep them calm while they all crossed the water. Everyone was tense and a little worried.

According to a quote from *The Wilsonian*, a family newsletter that was circulated amongst the family for many years:

"Soon everything was in place and Charlie led the big teams and wagons on to the swaying floor of the ferry. Anna and the boys stayed in the wagon. The boys had poor Bounce so trussed up he could hardly breath and gave out little whimpers of protest from time to time. The boys were completely awed by all the water around them. Anna had hated every minute on the big ship when she came from Germany and declared she would never get on a boat again! What was she doing on this creaking, heaving plank floor just sitting over the water?

The wind was whipping waves over the floor of the ferry and spray was soaking everything. Charlie had to hold the horses heads as they seemed to mistrust the whole situation. Soon the ferry pulled into the South Dakota river bank and were safely on their way again."

The whole family was weary as they moved along the next few days. Anna was especially tired. She was carrying their fourth child.

Charlie had a surprise when they finally reached the site of their new home—it was nothing like he had expected. There was only a small dilapidated shack on the property, built over a cave.

There was no well for water and there were no fences! It was a desolate and undeveloped property, unlike he had been led to believe that day in Sioux City when he'd proudly made his purchase. He was angry and bitterly disappointed.

He made alternative plans instantly. The next morning he traveled the sixteen miles to Kimball to get supplies and lumber for improvements on the shack over the cave so they would have a temporary shelter for living quarters.

On his return he repaired and improved the small shack and formulated a plan for his family during the coldest part of the winter—he was certain Anna could not stay in South Dakota with the baby due in late January or early February.

Charlie sent Anna and the boys by train to Omaha to stay with her sister Marie for the remainder of Anna's pregnancy. He promised to join them there in plenty of time for the birth, and hoped to find some carpenter work so he could stay there until spring.

TWO

Kate Arrives

CHARLIE AND ANNA'S first daughter was born February 11, 1909. Anna and the three boys were staying with Anna's sister Marie Otto and her family in Omaha, NE. The baby was not named immediately, and there was no certificate documenting her birth. In subsequent years Kate remembered hearing some comments regarding the sobriety of the doctor who attended the birth, and his professionalism or lack of.

About two weeks later Charlie and Anna named the new baby Kate Emma. When she was older, Kate thought her name sounded like one someone might give their horse, so she decided she would be called Kathryn and that name stuck. All of her official papers showed her legal name to be Kathryn, although informally she was still called "Kate" or "Katie." Perhaps this was the first sign of her independent streak; there were more to come.

Anna and the children stayed in Omaha for about a year after Kate's birth. Towards summer Charlie returned to South Dakota for a few months to do his farming and to make home improvements. He spent the winter months in Omaha again but returned to South Dakota early in the spring 1910 to prepare for the arrival of his family.

The spring weather was still brisk when the family arrived by train in Kimball. Charlie was there to pick them up and take them to their now-ready home. He was driving a classy team of horses pulling a double box wagon filled with hay and plenty of warm blankets for the 16-mile trek to the homestead. It was a long trip, especially for the children, and nearly nightfall when they arrived. Charlie and the older boys unpacked the wagon.

Kate in the buggy with her big brother Ira, 1909

Anna, Ira, and the baby were very tired so Anna fixed a place for them to sleep and they went to bed. Charlie warmed some stew he had prepared for Henry and Fred. The boys were starved and raved about how good the stew tasted as they devoured it with bread and butter. Charlie wanted them to be healthy, so he made sure he had milk for them to drink. They were tired from the trip, too. Charlie helped the boys get to bed. Tomorrow they would have lots of time to look around the farm.

The following morning the boys checked out everything, noting this appeared to be great country for flying kites. There was nothing for the kites to get tangled up in, not even trees, because it was all open country. Another thing they noticed was the nice green grass growing close to the house. Charlie found this amusing and informed them that by late summer that "green grass" would be ugly thistles with lots of stickers.

Their home was actually a cave under what had been that original old shack. It was quite warm and had one rock wall. Charlie had enlarged the building on top for future use but it wasn't quite ready to be occupied. It didn't take much fuel to heat the cave. Fuel was scarce and might be anything from cow chips to twisted hay or flax straw.

The cookstove had holes on the heating surface with removable lids where corn cobs or coal would normally be put down and burned. To burn straw, two old boilers were stuffed full of straw, one used immediately and the other to replace it when needed. The lids from the stove top were removed and the stuffed boiler was turned upside down over the burner hole. Through a small door on the side of the stove they could light the straw on fire. Flax straw was preferred because it burned hotter.

This story was told by Fred Wilson in *The Wilsonian:*

"I remember one time Mother sent me out to the pasture with a sack to pick up some nice dry cow chips so she could have a good fire to bake bread. As I was walking along with my eyes to the ground looking, I see a big jack rabbit

within a step of me so I thinks to myself 'we just as well have rabbit for supper.' So I jumped right on top of the rabbit and after I got aholt of him I was wondering how I could let him go for he was kicking me in the face and all over. When I got shed of that rabbit that was the last time I jumped on a rabbit. I did get the cow chips. I hoped they were dry."

THREE

Home Improvements

AT FIRST IT was somewhat problematic finding places for everyone to sleep in the little house on the Buffalo County homestead. With limited space, Charlie cleverly found a way for one bedroom to be down in the cave area. There was a dirt floor but one wall was rock which provided stability. Charlie fixed a trap door with a ladder to go between levels. At first Charlie and Anna slept down there with Katie and Ira, and the older boys slept upstairs. When Charlie added onto the main floor of the house—to make it more like a real house—they traded places, and the older boys slept downstairs.

Charlie used his creative skills to make more room for living upstairs. He built a bed that could be folded up into the wall during the day and folded out at night. This was where he and Anna slept. Today we call it a Murphy bed. Kate was impressed by how her dad had so cleverly designed the bed to look like a chest of drawers when folded up into the wall. Charlie found a corner on the main level for a baby bed for Kate, and another corner where Ira could sleep.

Charlie had a part-time hired hand by the name of George

Peterson who did planting and other work while Charlie did custom work for neighbors. George was a trustworthy, hard-working guy who had earned Charlie's respect. George lived at the Wilson homestead when he was needed for field work, and also helped with chores when Charlie was off doing construction work. Charlie's carpenter skills were in demand and that pay was good. He built houses and barns and repaired or remodeled many places in the area. It was a good way for him to supplement the family income until the crops were harvested, and it helped fund the addition onto their home. Kate spoke about her dad also doing custom work "making hay" for a lot of neighbors, meaning he cut, raked, and stacked hay for them.

Fred Wilson, Sr. later reported that the years 1914-1925 were pretty good for farming, but along with abundant moisture came a lot of thunderstorms, which terrified Anna. Fred, sensing his mother's nervousness, also became nervous about storms.

During one of these storms the family experienced a time of real terror. Charlie was off building a house for someone who lived near Vega, a small town about ten miles away. He camped there overnight part of the time and so did not always return home. George, the hired man, stayed at the homestead then and shared the cave bedroom with the older boys, Henry and Fred. Fred remembered a night when he was awakened by loud thunder and a feeling of extreme terror. He described the experience in the family newsletter *The Wilsonian*:

> *"What I am about to write happened in the middle of the night. George and Henry was sleeping in one bed and Ira and I was sleeping together in another bed and these two double beds were side by side. The heads of the beds were towards the rocked up wall. Lightning struck close to the house and I woke up scared and I started yelling, "CYCLONE! CYCLONE!" The screeching I was doing awakened George. He sat up in bed and he had no more than sat up when the side of the basement rock wall started to cave in, but George got out of the way. Henry and Ira was buried under the rock and dirt. The*

bedsteads were iron and they pushed forward on top of the boys. Henry was buried with more dirt and rock than Ira so Mother and George freed Henry first and in the meantime I managed to get a breath hole through to Ira's head so he could get air."

Fred didn't say how long it took to complete the rescue but it was a traumatic experience. When Charlie arrived home he was amazed at the damage. Anna was a small lady and not very strong but she was able to open the trap door to the basement, scramble down the ladder screaming for George to help her, and together they achieved the impossible—moving boulders and dirt off the boys trapped beneath.

Charlie said he couldn't imagine how they did it and it was nothing short of a miracle. Fred said later if he had not picked up on the fear of storms from his mother he probably would not have started screaming when he did. He really felt that the hand of God was in their rescue.

FOUR

More Babies

MARY ANNE WAS BORN at the Wilson homestead Sept 19, 1911. It is not clear, but either Dr. Tandy or Dr. McManus was in attendance for this birth. Surprisingly, there were two doctors practicing in this sparsely settled area at that time.

Kate remembered being told that when Charlotte was born, Mrs. Baltzer—a good friend and neighbor—was with Anna at the Wilson place. Mrs. Baltzer said to Anna, "Now, Mrs. Wilson, you have three boys and three girls." Kate laughed as she told this story and said, "I think she might have been suggesting to Anna that this would be a good time to stop with the babies." Still laughing, Kate added, "Well, two boys and one girl arrived later!"

All nine of the children were born healthy and, as far as we know, Anna never lost a baby.

The family managed to maintain good health throughout their growing years. I am sure the efficiency and planning on the part of that "little dynamo" Anna had a lot to do with that. Each child grew up knowing how to do a day's work. It took real administrative skill to keep a family that large organized. Everybody had jobs to do and each depended on others to do their own jobs also. This took teamwork and cooperation. Anna was often alone with the family when Charlie was off working for others, and she clearly demonstrated unusual abilities at organizing and multi-tasking. She was definitely the family CEO.

FIVE

Childhood Fun

KATE'S older brothers were quite creative. For winter fun they built a sled that their dog could pull. They also built a box on top of their sled, in which Kate rode. For the most part, it worked well and she enjoyed her rides, although she remembered tipping over and rolling in the snow many times. Her brothers picked her up, brushed the snow off her, put her back in the sled, and away they would go. Kate recalled being pulled to school quite often in that little homemade sled.

The children also spent many hours entertaining themselves on a pond located a short distance from the farmhouse. Henry and Fred had great fun with a raft they constructed by tying together tree branches. The raft had a barrel attached on top and they constructed poles from more tree branches to push the raft around the pond. Kate became a passenger inside the barrel and she recalled how she loved the rides with Henry and Fred as they floated from one end of the pond to the other. The pond eventually dried up and today there is no sign of it at the homestead.

When Kate, Mary, and Charlotte became bored being at home—especially in the summertime—they took long walks out in the pasture and often spent afternoons picking wildflowers and admiring their beauty. They played a game using the flower petals. After finding a flower they thought was appropriate, they would pluck it and think of a boy on whom they had a "crush." Then they would pick one petal off at a time while reciting "He loves me" and —picking another petal— "He loves me not" until there were no more petals on the flower. If the last petal was pulled as they said, "He loves me," that meant the boy loved them. They laughed until their sides hurt and teased each other about boys the rest of the day.

Kate recalled their favorite spot on top of a big boulder out in the pasture. The three girls climbed up on that big old rock and sang songs, taking turns choosing a song. All three sang at the top of their lungs such songs as "Darling Nelly Gray," "Old Black Joe," and some that were then of a more popular style such as "Jada Jada Jing Jing Jing."

The girls were great pretenders, and they created situations in which they pretended to be certain characters. Usually it was Charlotte who would say, "Now you 'tend like you're the mama and I'll 'tend like I'm the daddy. Mary, you be the little baby." They spent hours making up stories and role-playing.

Creativity seemed to come naturally to them. Clothespins—the kind that had a head on top and appeared to have two legs—became dolls, dressed as men or women. When the new Sears and Roebuck catalog arrived in the mail the girls hurried to pick out their favorite styles of clothes, and then cut out the pictures to dress their clothespin dolls. It was important to get this done before the catalog was relegated to the outhouse to be used as toilet paper. During the summer other clothes for their dolls were made from discarded husks of corn.

Speaking of the outhouse, Kate recalled that she was the one most often appointed to escort the younger children when the call came in that they "had to go." She was the oldest daughter, and when the time came she would hear Anna call, "Katie, you need to take Charlotte (or whomever) out to the toilet." Often it would be at night, and it was one of the scariest tasks she had to do. There were no flashlights in those days so she tried to get the dog to go with them; a lot of times he didn't want to go either. The call would also often come at meal time and she might then take more than one sibling at the same time. It was a real "drag." There were terrible drawbacks being the oldest girl in the family!

The Wilson sisters' behavior was very similar to that of young girls of today. On some occasions the three girls began to giggle while eating, for no apparent reason. All they needed to keep the giggles going was a glance at each other. Charlie and Anna sent them away from the table until they could "straighten up." When they received permission to return, they dared not look at each other or they would again burst into giggles. Sometimes they were sent away from the table more than once.

There were other times when the girls got a giggling streak about something, and their mother couldn't help joining in the laughter. She laughed as hard as the girls and, slapping her lap, she hooted, "Oh, you crazy kids!" (with her German accent, she rolled her r's). Kate could imitate her perfectly. The girls thought it a great time if they could get their mom to laugh with them. Anna was a good sport, in spite of working so hard and having so much responsibility raising nine kids. Kate fondly recalled many good laughs with her mother while growing up.

The ladies in the neighborhood took turns hosting social events in their homes for the other ladies. One incident Kate found amusing was a time when Anna hosted such an event and was preparing to entertain the ladies in the Wilson home.

The Web Marshall family owned a team of "high stepping bays" that pulled a fancy buggy with a fringed top. The Wilsons often admired the team and buggy as Web drove by their house each day on his way to the town of Gann Valley to work at the Buffalo County Courthouse. He offered up transportation for this special occasion if anyone thought they could handle his fancy prancing team of horses.

Julia Kopke thought she was horsewoman enough to handle the team and offered to pick up all the ladies and deliver them to the Wilson homestead for the event.

When Julia drove into the Wilson yard she could only keep the horses quiet for a short time. While the buggy was stopped at the Wilson's door, one lady carefully stepped out of the jiggling vehicle as the team pranced in place, straining at their bridles to be moving again. Julia talked to them in a soothing voice—"Whoa, Babe, whoa Prince"—then, as she slacked her grasp on the reins while a lady disembarked, she still had to restrain them enough to make a turn around the house to deliver another lady to the front door, hoping she could keep the horses still long enough for that lady to exit the buggy. Anna braced herself by the porch entrance to the house so she could assist the ladies who carefully and uncertainly stepped from the moving buggy to the porch.

When it was time to go home, Julia brought the buggy around to the door again where she picked up one lady at a time and followed the same process to deliver them back home.

Kate and her sisters watched the ladies in great anticipation of a misstep, going or coming. The kids were highly entertained, snickering and laughing, as they spied from a window inside the house, ready to enjoy whatever "action" might take place. The ladies disappointed the children—they all exited and entered the buggy successfully, with Anna's assistance.

The sisters talked about Julia and the "high stepping bays" years later and enjoyed a good laugh. They had no recollection of what Julia did with the team during the ladies event, but they felt sure keeping that team quiet for two hours or more, tied up and waiting for the return trip, had to be a huge challenge.

The Wilson brothers had inquisitive and curious minds and they became inventors of toys and games to entertain themselves and other family members. They built sleds and kites and constructed stilts for all the kids to walk on. They became skillful at moving fast enough on their stilts that they sometimes even played tag. Charlie, being the carpenter that he was, had some influence on them, showing them the process, the "how to," in creating these things. Anna, too, was creative and encouraged them by helping however she could.

Kate recalled that Anna would take time to join in the fun. She saved everything, so she could access her stash of used paper and rags to create something beautiful and fun.

Kites were favorites. Anna made a paste of flour and water to attach old newspaper or wrapping paper around the wooden framework that the boys constructed. Then she would find old rags to tie on the string for a kite tail so it would fly well when launched. Finding the right combination of rags for the tail was always a challenge, but also part of the fun.

When it all came together the kids would run into the wind with the kite in one hand and a ball of string in the other hand, releasing the kite slowly while it gracefully bobbed and swayed in the wind and rose into the sky. They could watch it for hours as they ran from place to place with the string in their hands. Sometimes, when it was tied to a fence post, it would stay in the air for several days, diving and floating as though doing a beautiful dance in the sky. Finally it wore out and dove back to earth, never to fly again. Kites were the best!

Each of Kate's brothers had a riding horse and on Sundays the neighborhood boys brought their horses to the Wilson homestead.

Then the boys rode around together all afternoon. Sometimes they had horse races, and in the winter they rode to Crow Creek to go ice skating.

All the boys trapped muskrats, skunks, and rabbits and sold the furs for spending money, which was always welcome.

The Wilson family lived near a freight and mail route. When the girls were bored at home they would hang out by their mailbox at the end of the lane when getting the mail to watch for the freighters to go by. A caravan of four to six wagons, pulled by several teams of horses, moved freight between the Kimball railroad depot and the town of Gann Valley several times each week. The road was made by the wagons but well-worn from constant travel. The ruts were deep, and some days Kate, Mary, and Charlotte would sit on the edge of the trail, burying their bare feet in the dirt at the bottom of the rut. They loved the feel of the warm dirt as they squiggled their toes in it. Other days they would just stand by the mailbox, waiting for the freighters so they could wave at them as they passed. The drivers always returned their wave. Eventually, the trail was graded and today is a paved highway known as South Dakota State Highway 45. It runs north and south connecting US I-90 to US Hwy 14, and still passes through Gann Valley.

When Kate was thirteen years old a man drove a pickup truck into their yard with a piano in the back. He said he was selling pianos and asked Charlie if he would like to buy one.

Charlie asked, "How much?"

The salesman said, "Thirty-five dollars."

Charlie said, "Unload it!"

Kate and her sisters were beyond thrilled. They jumped up and down, screaming and hugging each other. The piano furnished the music for house parties and dances in their living room for many years. The Wilson home became popular as a great place for house parties, with much singing and dancing. Charlie and Anna encouraged the parties since they, too, enjoyed the good times.

They played the piano by ear since none of them had taken lessons. Charlie couldn't afford to have the girls take lessons yet. Later, Kate had the privilege of having a few weeks of instruction at Springfield, when she attended high school there. She then helped the other girls learn some chords. The girls also picked up ideas from neighbor kids who did take lessons. Gradually, they could play a song with both hands, and then they started to have fun. Sometimes they assembled a kitchen band with the piano, and all in the family participated. They used a washboard, pan lids—and brother Ira played the bones. He saved beef or pork rib bones and would carefully clean off all the meat. Once dried, they were ready for him to put between his fingers and knock together in rhythm to the music. He became quite accomplished and was often called on to play at parties.

One childhood event that Kate attended made a big impression on her. She was given permission to go with brothers Henry, Fred, and Ira. Her dad gave her a quarter to spend. She was in awe of a beautiful merry-go-round which also made lovely music, thinking it the nearest thing to heaven there could be.

Its graceful horses moved like gentle waves on water on a beautiful day. The music was intriguing, like she imagined one would hear in heaven. After she spent her quarter to ride the merry-go-round, she found Henry and told him of her intense yearning to ride again, but she didn't have any more money. He took pity on her and gave her two more quarters. She was ecstatic and went back to the merry-go-round and spent it all on two more rides.

Kate thought this event might have been a Buffalo County Fair held in Gann Valley. She remembered everything set up in a pasture east of town. There were tents where she could view the handiwork of local women. Some tents had displays of grains and garden produce. Another tent showed off the accomplishments of school children, such as art and penmanship.

Kate remembered many Native Americans camped at this event. She observed interesting things about them. They had set up their teepees at the north end of the fairgrounds. They brought their families and pets with them by wagon, and she observed lots of activity among the children and their dogs. She also noticed each teepee had a campfire in front of it. Kate was aware there was a reservation somewhere in the area but she had never had any interaction with the people who lived there. She was fascinated and filled with curiosity about them and watched them for a long time.

Education at Elementary School

GETTING an education was quite a challenge in the early 1900s on the plains of South Dakota. When Kate and her siblings were old enough they attended a small one-room school near their home. There were three windows on one side of the school, and portraits of George Washington and Abraham Lincoln prominently adorned the upper opposite wall, underneath of which was a blackboard. The teacher's desk, a recitation bench where students discussed their assignments with the teacher, and another blackboard were situated in the front. Each school had a large pot-bellied stove, fed with coal.

Desks were built for two students, with room enough inside for each to place school supplies and books. When Kate started school there was no desk for her so the teacher assigned her to sit between Henry and Fred, her older brothers. She felt crowded, and had no place for her books.

Every township had its own school board that hired and/or fired the teacher, based on their own selective performance criteria. Wages were set by the board without using a pay scale of any kind, and rules for the teachers were set by these boards. Usually the mothers of the school children got together before classes started in the fall to clean the building thoroughly, and paint it if they thought it was needed.

One year the school board hired a teacher who was certified to teach ninth graders. Henry Wilson, Faith and Vina Gaulke, and Gertrude Stroud were in that class. The following year, those students were then allowed to enter high school in Gann Valley as tenth graders.

It was common in rural communities for the boys to attend school for only two or three months of the year since they were expected to help plant in the spring and harvest crops in the fall. It was not unusual for boys sixteen years of age to still be attending school for a few months each year. These older boys sometimes became behavior problems by challenging the rules set by the teacher, and by bullying other children. Kate didn't remember any of the boys being bullies in her school.

Not far from the school that the Wilson children attended there was a high peaked hill that the students called Pikes Peak. It was their favorite place to slide downhill on their sleds in the winter. In the spring the teacher hiked with them to the peak and they all picked crocus flowers. The crocus blossoms were the first sign that spring had arrived. They were beautiful little pink flowers that bloomed early, often through the snow. The students also ran up and down the hill, and sometimes even rolled down the hill. They felt a new surge of energy with the season of spring.

When the students returned to the school with the crocuses they placed them in empty ink bottles they had saved during the year. Each desk was adorned with fresh crocus blossoms to remind them that spring had arrived.

Kate loved flowers from the time she was very young and remembered how they made the schoolroom look beautiful. She expressed how she loved the way the flower was a beautiful orchid color, light on the outside to deep purple in the middle. She noted the delicate the little stamens in the middle that were yellow in contrast to the purple. She recalled thinking, "No one but God could design a thing of such great perfection and beauty."

As an adult, Kate often marveled at the beauty of nature. She often commented on the simple things in nature: the beauty of a corn field; a garden with rows of vegetables; the clouds in the sky; or forests and mountains. She praised God for the beauty of this earth almost every day.

Among Kate's humorous recollections of grade school are playing in the rolling hills in a pasture near the school playground. One of the students was an older boy with mental limitations. He was the child of a neighbor family with whom the Wilsons frequently visited, and the children often played together at one home or the other. At school the boys sometimes excluded this boy from their games but he was welcome to join the girls in their games.

When the girls were playing in the hills behind the schoolhouse, this boy chased them while flailing his arms wildly, making wild growling noises, pretending he was a roaring dragon. He threatened to spit fire on them and devour them, and maybe destroy the whole earth. The girls ran up and down the hills, screaming at the top of their lungs, pretending to escape the fate of fire spat upon them by the dragon. Kate laughed telling the story and was sure that their game provided ample exercise.

Sometimes they played more organized games such as Anti-I-Over. All ages could participate in this game. The school was rather small so the requirement of throwing the ball over the roof to the other side was possible, even for the smaller children. They chose sides for two teams, with a team on each side of the schoolhouse. One team threw the ball over the roof of the school calling "Anti-I-Over." If the ball was caught by someone on the opposite side, the catching team would race around the school without warning and try to tag as many players as possible on the opposite side. Tagged players then joined the opposing team; in a sense they were captured. If no one caught the ball on the other side, they then threw it back over the building and the same action took place with the opposing team. The object was to capture the entire opposing team to become winner of the game. Kate did not recall teachers supervising play on the playground during recesses.

Another memory was a story about one of the older girls who had an altercation with the teacher. The girl became quite angry and refused to obey the teacher. She went to the cloak room, got her coat, and left. Later the girl returned with word that her siblings were to gather up their books and go back home with her. She informed the teacher that her mother would teach them at home. Kate didn't think those kids ever returned to school, and remarked that "the school was a whole lot more peaceful like that, anyway!" She further commented, "That girl had caused a lot of trouble for the teacher and also the other children, which no doubt was a reflection of the attitude of the mother."

There always seemed to be some kind of pecking order on the school grounds. In Kate's school the students whose families were better off financially were the playground leaders. They would particularly note the color of Kate's red hair, or that she might be physically weak. They taunted her and goaded her into a physical challenge with a much weaker and smaller child, and then when she was winning the challenge the rest of the girls stepped in to help the smaller child who was losing. Then later they ridiculed Kate about how she could not measure up to a younger, weaker child. On some of those occasions her older brothers, Henry and Fred, came to her rescue and the girls scattered, knowing they had no chance against the "big boys."

Some of these things are timeless and universal. It seems bullying has been around since the beginning of time and has caused some people a lot of pain. Kate had her ways of coping and eventually, of course, the troublemakers graduated and were gone.

I have heard it said that what doesn't kill us makes us stronger, and in Kate's case I believe it truly applied. Anna, the little child whom Kate was often goaded into challenging, eventually became her good friend, and they maintained their friendship until Anna's death.

When the family lived on the Sobek place—because the Wilson homestead didn't have water for a couple of years— the Wilson kids attended a different school. Kate thought she might have been in second grade, and she was the only girl in that school. Kate and one of the Wolff boys were the same age, and those parents were good friends with the Wilsons. The neighborhood boys often invited each other to stay overnight at one home or the other and Kate felt like she got cheated out of all the good times because she was never invited. On one of those occasions Mrs. Wolff did invite Kate to stay overnight. She had fun playing games with her friend and classmate who happened to be a boy. Mrs. Wolff made a special bed for her to sleep in so she could have her own private bedroom, and made a nice lunch for her to take to school the next day. Kate recalled thinking how important she felt. She thought Mrs. Wolff was a very special lady when she shared this memory.

School supplies in those days included such things as a tablet, pencil, and ink pen which required a bottle of ink. The ink bottles were never thrown away. The teacher found some use for them, such as a vase for the crocuses each spring following a long, hard winter. Parents were expected to buy books for their children at the county school superintendent's office.

Each child was expected to take a lunch to school with them for the noon break. Usually they took some kind of sandwich and a cookie. At certain times of the year they were lucky enough to have fresh fruit such as an apple, or perhaps some vegetable they could eat raw. The lunches were often packed in a recycled gallon-sized syrup can. The family always had pancakes for breakfast so Mom Wilson accumulated the necessary pails. Their names were on the buckets. Most all of the students had lunch pails like the Wilson kids.

Kate spoke highly of Mrs. Benedict, who taught at one of the schools the Wilson children attended. She taught each of the Wilson children from Ira down during her tenure at that school. Mrs. Benedict drove by their home every day in her fancy "one-horse shay"—which was a small buggy—no matter how cold or warm the weather. The Benedicts were a bit wealthier than others in the community, so Mrs. Benedict was well dressed, and her horse and shay looked very classy. She was the picture of professionalism and very proper. Kate remembered her as a wonderful teacher and a very gracious and refined lady.

A quote from Charlotte Wilson Erickson describes a school scene with Mrs. Benedict in *The Wilsonian*:

"Christmas was a very special time. Our school teacher worked very hard to give all the students pieces to learn and plays to be in. Every recess we would practice our parts, and the week before the big day we practiced half of every day. We really liked that. Our teacher would fix the front part of our school for a stage. She would string wire from one side to the other and drape sheets over the wire so we could pull them in between acts of our play. There were about sixteen of us students. Finally the big day arrived. Mom worked so hard so we kids could all look nice. Dad had the horses hitched to the sleigh with jingle bells tied to their harnesses, and as we drove along we loved the sound of the constant jingle. Mom heated bricks and wrapped them in old towels and put them in the sleigh to keep us warm. Dad had put nice clean straw on the floor. Our sleigh had benches on both sides for us to sit on. We

put horse blankets on our laps to keep us warm, and sometimes we would put them on our heads if it was snowing.

Mom, along with the other parents, would make popcorn balls for a treat after the program. I remember looking all the parents over and thinking that my dad and mom were the very best- looking ones there.

On Christmas Eve we would hang up our stockings. It was so much fun to get up on Christmas Day to find out what our parents had put in our stockings. Usually it would be an apple or an orange, and of course, candy. And we could get clothes like long-legged underwear. At that time of the year my folks always got from Montgomery Wards a big pail of candy, a box of fig cookies, and large seedless raisins. That pail of candy, which was one of the highlights, was divided into four sections. Three I remember: peanut brittle, ribbon candy, and soft chocolates. Our parents worked very hard to make our Christmas really special.

I've brought out a few precious memories. My folks loved to help others. They were honest, respectful, and knew how to work hard. We learned a lot from them."

SEVEN

Farm Chores

EVERY DAY KATE and her sisters walked to the pasture to bring the cows home to be milked. One cow was extra gentle and the girls discovered they could ride her so they frequently took turns riding the cow home from the pasture. One afternoon, though, something spooked the cows and they suddenly started to run. Kate was riding the tame cow and she fell off, landing with the full force of her body on her elbow. She walked home in severe pain, holding up her dangling broken arm. A doctor in Gann Valley was called to come examine Kate's arm. Dad Wilson returned home about the same time as the doctor arrived, and helped set the broken arm. Since she received no sedative and her arm was broken in the elbow joint, it was an extremely painful procedure for Kate.

In about a week, when Kate was feeling better, the teasing began.

"How did you break your arm?"

Kate replied "Oh, I fell off a cow."

Then the girls would break into gales of laughter.

The truth is, because the arm was broken at the elbow joint, it took a very long time to heal. Kate never recovered to the extent that it was normal, but it became fairly functional and she was able to use it. She was always thankful for no ongoing pain and she never developed arthritis in the joint.

Everybody pitched in to help get work done on the farm. Even the girls had to know how to milk cows. Kate was very young when she learned how to perform this daily chore. Her two younger sisters, Mary and Charlotte, also eventually had to learn this "art form."

The cows were herded into the corral and the "milkers approached the bossy cow with stool in one hand and pail in the other. Sometimes the cow did not wish to be milked at that particular time. It often required some gentle persuasion to "park her" in a convenient place where the milker could make contact with the milkee. The stool was frequently used as a threat toward the animal, but being a three-legged affair of rather sturdy wood that seemed a bit absurd—the girls were barely strong enough to carry the stool in one hand with their pail in the other. Verbiage was their main threat toward the cow if she was uncooperative; and sometimes it didn't sound like girl talk. The girls were sure the cow comprehended what she needed to do at their direction. That may have been true; but if so, the cows often pretended not to hear. Once the milker was seated by the cow, and proceeded with the process of extracting milk, the cow might feel the need to move to a different position. This sometimes resulted in the pail of milk being knocked over by an unpredictable hoof, which in turn caused tears, and terrible names to be shouted at the cow. It wasn't good enough to shout from the milking position; the girls felt they had to shout into the ear of the cow.

On more joyful occasions with the cows, the girls squirted milk at the mouths of the cats that gathered around waiting for a treat.

The game was to see who could squirt milk directly into the mouths of the cats the most times. No one knew how much milk landed on the fur of the cat or just hit the dirt. Sometimes the squirted milk just "accidentally" landed on one of the other girls, thereby starting a milk squirting fight, with screams and giggling that alerted Anna to what was happening. After a firm scolding they got back to work.

Some things are universal and timeless. These kids were no different in their mischievous antics than those who came before or after them.

After the cows were milked the girls hauled the pails of milk to the house where the milk was run through the cream separator. It had a big bowl-shaped container into which the raw milk was poured. The bowl was a steel structure which was set on four feet and stood about four feet tall. When the handle of the separator was cranked, the cream ran out of a spout and the blue fatless milk —skim milk—would come out another spout. It was important to turn the handle at a certain speed because the separator used centrifugal force in order to separate the milk from the cream. Most of the cream was sold to supplement household income and used to purchase groceries; however, Anna always held back some cream for cooking, and for making special treats.

The orphan calves were "pail fed," usually the skim milk.

When Kate was ten or eleven years old the chicken chores were assigned to her. She gathered the eggs daily, kept straw in the hens' nests where they laid eggs, and cleaned the chicken house—which included painting the chicken roosts with kerosene to get rid of lice and mites.

In late spring some of the hens got "broody" and wanted to "set." When the hens got a little cranky and complained to Kate by picking at her with their beaks when she reached under them to gather their eggs, she knew she should prepare a place for them to "set."

She placed these hens in straw-filled boxes in another shed. If they accepted one or two eggs that Kate placed under them, they became part of a group called the "setting hens." This meant the hen was resigned to "setting" on several eggs for three weeks, only getting out of the box to eat and drink. Kate was fascinated with the behavior of the hens because they were so loyal to their purpose; and she found it amazing that each hen knew exactly where her box was located, and returned to that box after eating. At the end of three weeks, adorable fluffy chicks miraculously hatched out of the eggs.

Kate marveled at this miracle of life and also at how proud the hens were of their babies. She was amazed at the hens' instinct to protect their chicks. The sight of the baby chicks melted Kate's heart and she dearly loved each one of them.

Following the hatch, the hens and their babies were moved to a separate little building called a coop. There were vertical stakes at the door of the coop that allowed the chicks to get out, but not the mother hens. If the mother was allowed to take her babies where she wanted, she might wander into tall grass where the babies couldn't get around and might get lost. If the mother hen was limited to movement only in the coop then the babies would stay close by her as she "talked" to them. When the chicks got older and grew bigger, the hens were allowed to go out with them and they all roamed the yard together.

Kate loved to see the mother with her babies following her. She observed that when the mother found a treasure to eat she called for the little ones and they would come running to her for their treat. When the chickens were fully grown, the males were killed for eating, leaving only a few roosters as part of the brood. Kate was very observant of their behavior, in awe of the whole process, from hatching to when the chicks became adults.

Charlie and Anna also raised turkeys on their farm, and Kate and some of the her siblings fed and watered them daily. One morning when Kate went out to feed the turkeys she saw feathers flying and heard lots of turkey gobbling west of the house, near the pond. She went to investigate the commotion. A turkey hen was trying to protect her babies from a coyote that was attacking them. The coyote had pulled feathers out of her back and raw flesh was exposed. Kate ran toward the coyote, waving her arms and shouting, to scare it away.

The mother turkey had warned the little ones and they had very cleverly hidden themselves in the tall grass. When the coyote was gone she found them in the grass and stayed with them until she was sure it was safe again. Kate loved the little bright-eyed baby turkeys.

Kate had respect for all of God's creatures and admired how the mothers protected and cared for their little offspring. She often remarked about how animals, wild and tame, have a capacity to love and protect their babies, just like humans—a belief that I carry with me to this day.

There were a lot of coyotes near the Wilson place. Kate spoke about hearing the coyotes howling at night. They had a weird kind of yell, by yipping a few times, followed by a long, shrill, high pitched, blood-curdling howl. The family dog answered them by howling similarly. This had a chilling effect on Kate and she covered her head with a pillow hoping not to hear them. After a long time she finally fell asleep with the coyotes still howling.

EIGHT

Fall Harvest

CHARLIE RAISED some grain crops but the harvest that Kate remembered best was the navy bean and corn harvest. Her brothers helped their dad pull up the navy bean vines in the fall and load them into a wagon. When the wagon was full, the boys crawled into the it and trampled the vines with their feet, throwing the chaff to the wind. They usually got several 50-lb. bags of beans to store for use over the winter. When Anna wanted to use the beans, she soaked a couple handfuls in water overnight, to be used later. Bean soup with pork was a staple in their family.

Kate helped her dad pick out corn for seed, choosing large ears with uniform straight rows of bright yellow kernels. The smaller kernels at the end of the ears were shelled off. Charlie always used his own seed for planting unless he didn't raise corn that year. The common yield for corn in those days amounted to twenty-five or thirty bushels per acre.

When it was time to harvest the corn crop, Charlie put an extra board on one side of his wagon which was called the "bang board." His team of horses slowly pulled the wagon down the row, while he plucked the ears of corn from the corn stalk and threw them against the "bang board" and into the wagon. Most farmer's teams were well trained and they responded to commands of "giddap" and "whoa" without anyone in the wagon holding the reins.

Kate recalled hearing her dad talk to the horses as they moved back and forth, and the sound of the ears of corn hitting the "bang board" from dawn until night. How much a man could pick each day was a matter of pride, and sometimes the farmer didn't stop picking all day, except for a quick sandwich for lunch.

NINE

Big Day for Anna

WHEN KATE WAS GROWING up in Buffalo County her parents never had a phone. If they needed to call someone they just went to the neighbor's house to use their phone. Charlie considered telephones more of a luxury than a necessity. Kate remembered, though, that her family always received a daily newspaper. She thought her dad was well read and understood what was going on all over the country, and the world. She admired his desire for knowledge about current events. He loved to read, and was interested in a wide range of topics. Even though he rarely had enough time to read the complete newspaper, he would never think of being without one.

Charlie felt that women should have the right to vote and was waiting for the day that Anna could go with him to the school and cast her vote. He watched the news carefully, and when that day arrived, he said, "Anna, today is voting day, so put on a clean apron and get your coat; you are going to be one of the first women in the country to vote!"

That day, in 1920, the family watched proudly as Charlie took Anna with him to the school to cast her vote. Charlie was clearly gratified that his wife could now join him in this important patriotic duty. His patriotism had a profound influence on his children.

Kate always felt a strong pride in being an American and, from an early age, understood the importance of justice and equality of women with men in our democracy. She was never shy about saying so.

TEN

Local Trade Centers

WHILE CHARLIE and Anna were raising their family in Buffalo County, they shopped in Vega, South Dakota and in Gann Valley. The towns were similar in size but in opposite directions from the Wilson farm. Few people have heard of Vega, but it was once a thriving little town. According to Kate's memory, Vega had a grocery store with a dance hall on the second story, and there was a time when beer was for sale on the second story. Vega also had a dry goods store, a John Deere implement dealer where Charlie purchased machinery, a bank, and a post office. At one time there was a creamery and cheese factory in Vega. Kate didn't remember other stores but she thought there was a church and a school. Charlie preferred to take the cream and eggs to Vega because they paid a little more for the farmers' products.

Kate attended a performance by Chautauqua players in Vega once. She described a large tent with seating constructed using wooden planks placed over supports that were similar to nail kegs. Kate thought the tent was enormous, in the eyes of a child. She remembered a stage where performers portrayed a historical character and was enthralled with what they had to say. She had a special interest in history at this early age and never lost that.

When Kate taught history in elementary school, she was able to explain historical events in story form to her students. They commented later that her teaching style enabled them to remember names and dates more easily, and they remembered the information longer. She made it interesting and her students responded in a positive way. Her dad seemed to recognize these creative qualities in Kate early in her life. Perhaps her Chautauqua experience made a lasting impression.

Gann Valley was also a thriving small town, with a grocery store also selling dry goods, more than one bank, cafes, a hardware store, implement dealer, hotel, school, post office, a church, and doctors.

At one time the town had high hopes that the railway line would go through, but that didn't materialize. The rail company chose to go through Miller, located about twenty-five miles north of Gann Valley.

A Visit to Grandparents

WHEN THE CHILDREN were still quite young, Charlie suggested that Anna take Kate, Mary, Charlotte, and Emil to visit his parents in Kansas. According to Fred Wilson—Kate's older brother—Anna was not enthusiastic about traveling on the train with all those young children (ages 10, 7, 5, and 2). Charlie suggested they stay for two or three weeks and visit relatives whom the children wouldn't remember or had never met, and whom Anna hadn't seen for several years. Anna wondered if the relatives would have room to accommodate them all? And what if they didn't all get along well? She had doubts, but finally agreed. Soon she and the children were on the train to Canton, Kansas from Kimball, South Dakota.

Kate felt hesitant and anxious about traveling by train. She didn't know what to expect. She had heard negative comments regarding train travel. The smell of smoke from time to time was unpleasant and the seats were uncomfortable. Mother Wilson depended on Kate's help with the younger children. It was difficult at first getting the little ones settled down, but eventually everyone adjusted to the train, its noise, smoke, and the other travelers. They moved from one car to another to eat meals, and the children slept on the train seats. Kate doubted Anna got much rest at all. Surprisingly, Kate found the trip a pleasant experience, with a few exceptions—most of those revolving around caring for a two-year-old.

Kate couldn't remember who met them at the train in Kansas, but they traveled to the home of her grandparents where they planned to stay. Kate recalled that Grandpa Wilson had a long beard and sat in an easy chair all the time without talking to the grandkids. They thought he seemed very stern. Grandma Wilson was good-natured—a small, petite, spritely little woman. She was friendly, down to earth, and always busy in the kitchen.

Kate's grandparents lived in a cottage style house where Grandma Wilson cooked wonderful meals on her kitchen range. Aunt Lena Ingram (their daughter) lived with them and she seemed friendly, but was always busy helping Grandma. Aunt Lena's children were grown at that time.

The children were pleased when they went to visit Uncle Jim and Aunt Sylvia for a few days because they had children—Eva, Violet, and identical twins Lloyd and Floyd. The cousins all got along quite well, but Kate remembered thinking the twins were "little devils" all the time.

Aunt Sylvia sewed red plaid dresses for Kate, Mary, and Charlotte. Kate thought herself beautiful, and felt like a princess in her new brightly colored dress. Aunt Sylvia was a jolly, wonderful, big-hearted lady. The children loved her. Kate was also very impressed with the huge apple orchard at their place.

Next they went to see Uncle Ira and Aunt Mayme and their family. Their children were Milton, Opal, and Ruby. Being about the same age as Kate, Ruby was blind and also had a neurological disorder that caused her to seem like she was angry; she banged her head on the floor. She always sat on the floor, and a St. Bernard dog was her constant companion. Kate was overcome with pity for Ruby when she saw her condition and her helplessness. She recalled sobbing because she felt so sorry for Ruby the first time she saw her; and then thought she embarrassed everyone by crying. She felt better when they assured her it was okay to cry. She tried to be especially nice to Ruby, and wanted to help her whenever she could. Ruby's parents told Kate that Ruby had experienced a very high fever with diphtheria and it had caused her to be blind and also damaged her brain. Ruby died when she was fifteen years old. Kate's experience with Ruby left a lasting impression. She later remarked that she wanted to help children who were like Ruby.

Early Charlie and Anna Wilson family: L-R Mary age 5; Charlotte age 3 (sitting); Kate age 7; Emil age 6 months. About 1916-1917.

One day, while visiting in Kansas, the family had an opportunity to go to the train depot when a troop train was passing through town. It was the summer of 1918 and the United States was heavily committed to World War I. There were hundreds of people at the train station waving and cheering for the soldiers that passed through the station. This made a big impression on Kate. She didn't fully understand the war but she was aware that nearly everyone wanted to show their support to the soldiers. She and the rest of the family joined in the celebration with great gusto.

While they were yelling and cheering, some children from the community said that the Wilson children shouldn't be cheering for the soldiers because "you don't live here." That made Kate feel scared and sad. She wanted to be part of the fun and excitement. She told her cousin Opal about it, who said, "You have as much right to cheer for the soldiers as anybody else." Kate felt relieved and happily rejoined the celebration, shouting and singing.

Mother Wilson decided to visit her former neighbors from Missouri before returning to South Dakota, and as the Wilson family changed trains at Kansas City, Kate observed some things she never forgot. She commented on how crowded the depot was, and observed many people being transported on stretchers covered with white sheets. She recalled that the flu epidemic was going on and she thought many of these people were gravely ill; and perhaps some were wounded soldiers from the war. She felt sad and uncomfortable because it was especially quiet and everyone was very serious, but she didn't understand why. She didn't ask questions then and it seems it was never discussed, leaving her feeling uncomfortable about it. It left an impression she never forgot. She was uncomfortable speaking about the event, even as an adult.

On their return trip to South Dakota from Missouri, the family stopped in Omaha, Nebraska to visit Anna's sister, Marie, and her family. Aunt Marie and Anna had always been close and they had not visited for a very long time. The Otto home was small but very modern. Anna and the children were treated royally. Uncle Gus and Aunt Marie only had one son, and they owned a grocery store. Uncle Gus brought home cheese and cold cuts every day—a rare treat for the Wilson children. They never ate such wonderful food at home. Kate thought her Uncle Gus must be very rich!

The family had an opportunity to ride on a street car to a

parade in downtown Omaha. The Wilson children thought that was a very special experience. The car was similar to a train but much cleaner and quieter. Kate was sure they would never see a street car in Gann Valley!

The family returned to Kimball from Omaha by train. Charlie was so ready for them to come home. He had really missed them. The trip turned out to be one that was unforgettable, and was really their only chance to get to know their Kansas relatives. Kate often spoke about the time they spent in Kansas as children.

TWELVE

Keeping Nine Looking Fine

WATER WAS a precious commodity in those early years, especially in the house. The family carried water from the well by hand for drinking, washing hands or bathing, and for washing clothes. A water pail was kept on the wash stand with a wash basin and soap. A pail containing water for drinking was also kept on the wash stand, with a dipper, from which the entire family drank— along with anyone else who might be at the house. Kate remarked, "It was a wonder that any of us lived with everyone drinking from the same cup." It was also common for a dipper to hang freely from a makeshift hook on the framework of the farm windmill in those days. The pump would supply cool water, fresh from the well, to anyone who wanted it—and everyone drank from the same dipper there too.

Keeping nine children in decent-looking clean clothes was a challenge. Doing the family wash was a big deal. First, water was hauled by hand in buckets from the pump outdoors, or pulled up one pail at a time from the cistern to heat in a large container called a boiler on the kitchen range in the house. It was common to have a cistern—an underwater tank or reservoir to catch and store rainwater for household purposes, such as washing clothes or cleaning. Cistern water was not used for drinking except in an emergency.

The rainwater was soft water and more desirable for use in washing clothes. Anna had a rain barrel to collect rainwater as it ran off the roof of the house, but it didn't rain frequently in Buffalo County so the barrel didn't always contain water. Sometimes, when there was snow, Anna sent the kids out to get snow to melt on the range for washing clothes because that water was also soft. If they used water from a well it was almost always hard water and lye would be used to soften the water.

The process for washing clothes involved using two big tubs, one having suds in it where the scrubbing took place. Very often Ira was the lucky one who did the scrubbing. He had to rub each garment up and down on a rough surface, usually a scrubbing board, or rub the fabric together to remove soil on the garment. The second tub was used to rinse the clothes and wring them out as dry as possible. All the wringing was done by hand at first, but later the family purchased a ringer. The ringer was a contraption that had two rollers tightly clamped together with a handle to turn at one end. One person would turn the handle and another person ran the wet clothes between the rollers to squeeze out the excess water. The wringer usually got more of the water out than wringing by hand, and was easier.

Next, someone had to haul the clean clothes out to the clothesline where they were secured to the line by clothespins, to hang in the breeze to dry. Sometimes the wet clothes would hang all afternoon on the line. In the winter the clothes were gathered to bring indoors by late afternoon; they might be frozen stiff, and even though not completely dry they smelled clean and fresh. The clothes would then be hung indoors, everywhere around the house, to finish drying.

Anna didn't have an ironing board so she folded a blanket on the table and ironed clothes on that. Since there was no such thing as easy-care fabric or electric dryers, nearly everything needed to be ironed.

She used what was called a flat iron. Anna had two or three flat irons that she placed on the kitchen stovetop to heat, and they had to get very hot. The children had to gather cobs for fuel to feed the kitchen range until the ironing was finished. Anna placed a handle on one of the irons, carried it to her homemade ironing board, and ironed until the iron lost its heat. Then she returned it to the stove top to re-heat, removed the handle and attached it to another iron, which had been heating while she ironed, and repeated this process many times until all the ironing was completed. Anna tested the iron for the degree of heat using the "spit" test. She would spit on her fingertips and touch the bottom of the iron very quickly so she wouldn't get burned. If she could hear the iron sizzle from spit on her fingers it was an indication the iron was hot enough. If it didn't sizzle, it had to be replaced on the stovetop until it passed the test.

The person doing the ironing—most often Anna—found this to be a rather tiring chore, especially in the summertime when it was hot outdoors and in the house. Because several people needed to be involved, ironing was one of the most dreaded chores. Anna would have been so happy to have a real ironing board, and she appreciated the electric irons developed after the children were grown.

One day, when Kate was about twelve years old, she was delegated by Anna to become the seamstress to sew dresses for the younger girls. Kate said, "Mom gave me the fabric and said I should sew a dress for Charlotte." Her mother informed Kate that she didn't have time to sew the girls' dresses, and she was sure Kate could handle it. Kate said, "Mom gave me the fabric and said I should sew a dress for Charlotte." Kate recalled feeling absolutely "scared to death that she would ruin the fabric and the dress would not be wearable." She didn't want to be wasteful! Apparently, Anna told her to take apart one of Charlotte's old dresses to use for a pattern for the new dress. With a few other instructions on sewing she became a seamstress. She remembered a high degree of stress sewing the first dress, but eventually she became quite good at sewing and really enjoyed it.

Sometimes flour sacks were available with a print on them and some women used the sacks as fabric to make dresses for their daughters. The prints were attractive and it made sense to recycle the sacks; and it saved money, too.

THIRTEEN

Hog Tragedy

KATE TOLD about an event that was devastating to Charlie and also had an effect on the family. She didn't remember the year but she thought she might have been about twelve years old. Livestock prices were good and Charlie was planning to pay all his bills and have some money left over; he was raising about two hundred hogs that year and had made big plans.

The hogs were growing into wonderful-looking specimens and he was sure they would bring an excellent price at the sale barn. He fed them with great care and checked on them often. He was very proud of them and had high hopes for this hog crop.

But the hogs suddenly and mysteriously contracted a disease called Hog Cholera. At that time there was no way to treat the disease and the hogs began to die. It was a dreadful experience for the family, to watch helplessly while the hogs just dropped dead one by one! All the hard work and money invested in feed was destroyed by this terrible disease. In just a matter of days, Charlie's hopes and dreams died with those hogs.

The dead hogs had to be disposed of because of fear the disease could spread. What could be done with two hundred dead hogs?

Charlie built a fire and began to burn the carcasses. Kate vividly remembered the sickening smell and, most of all, the extreme sadness they all felt. It took days to burn the carcasses, and each day was a new reminder of the total decimation of the dream to finally get ahead. Kate had never seen her father so sad. She desperately wanted to comfort him but felt helpless, and also hopeless. She remembered feeling sick herself because of this tragedy. Those were dark days for the family. They faced a large debt and there would be much loss of income, with no chance to pay down the debt.

But Charlie and Anna had to keep going. They couldn't just quit. After all, they had a family of nine children who had to eat. It meant picking themselves up, dusting themselves off, and starting all over again. And they did.

Charlie and Anna Wilson were beautiful role models for their children, exemplifying how to never quit, never give up, and never lose hope. They didn't quit. They *stayed in the buggy.* Kate remembered Anna telling Charlie, "It's ok, Charlie. Next year it vill be better." The kids heard that phrase many times from Anna as they grew up. Anna was a great supporter, always telling the family to look forward to times when "things would get better." She was always the family cheerleader.

FOURTEEN

Memories of World War I

*"Kaiser Bill went up the hill to get a look at France.
Kaiser Bill came down the hill with bullets in his pants."*

THIS WAS a popular saying during WWI when the United States was at war with Germany. Some songs that were popular were "Over There," "K-K-K-Katy," and "Johnny Get Your Gun."

Kate was about nine years old when the United States declared war on Germany in 1918. She remembered that the German language had been taught in some schools prior to the United States getting involved in the war. When the war started, schools dropped anything related to Germany, including speaking the language.

Anna's sister Dora and her daughter Toots from Omaha visited in the Wilson home during the war. One evening during supper an argument erupted regarding whether Germany or the United States was right. Dora believed that Germany was right and was adamant in her belief. Since Charlie was a True Blue American, he quickly stood up for America. Kate remembered some shouting across the table but her mother sternly interfered and stopped the argument. She forbade bringing up the war again and everyone agreed not to argue anymore, but they still kept their own beliefs about it. Anna was fine with "just don't talk about it."

Grandma and Grandpa Gaulke were neighbors to the Wilsons. Like Kate's mother Anna, they had migrated from Germany. Anna learned to talk and read and write English. Grandpa Gaulke could speak English but Grandma Gaulke could not, so Anna frequently visited the Gaulke home to visit with Grandma Gaulke in German. Anna felt that Grandma Gaulke must have gotten terribly lonely with no one to talk with.

Kate remembered an incident that her dad witnessed in Gann Valley during the war. He said Grandpa Gaulke was in a conversation with some guys about the war. He was upholding the Germans. They picked him up and threw him into the water tank, telling him that he was "all wet!"

Charlie told the family about it when he returned home with a load of lumber he had purchased. He said he pitied Mr. Gaulke and helped him out of the tank, but he also found the incident to be funny and he told about it through his laughter.

Sons Grow Up

CHARLIE THOUGHT Henry and Fred needed to learn some responsibility when they were about twelve and fourteen years old so he took them along on a custom farming job nearby. He had been hired to put up hay for a neighbor. Charlie and the boys took a tent to sleep in and enough food from home to get them through two or three days. This expedition was designed to be a lesson in camping and a work experience.

When they arrived home again, Charlie told Anna that just managing those boys kept him busy, and that they were such "roughnecks" that they kept breaking the machinery, so he spent most of his time repairing what they broke. He said, "They never took care of anything!" Many times Kate told stories, through her laughter, about her dad always making repairs to machinery, always fixing something those guys had broken, while they were supposed to be "helping" him.

Henry's first real job came from Rich Gaulke, who owned a quarter of land near the Wilson ranch. When Rich was planting corn he hired Henry to walk behind him and drop the corn in the furrows as he plowed them. Rich paid Henry thirty-five cents per day.

According to Jennie Wilson, Henry's wife, he started working for a family named Schooley after he finished grade school. The Schooleys farmed reservation land near the Wilson home. Henry was making hay for them. First he mowed the grass with a horse-drawn mower with a sickle only about eight feet wide. Then he used a hay rake, also pulled by the horses, to rake the grass into windrows (bunches of hay) for collection. Finally, the hay was collected in a hay rack and taken to the farm to be stored in the haymow (the upper story of the barn) or made into a haystack out in the field. This method of making hay was time-consuming and very hard work, especially if you worked alone. Pitchforking the hay into the hay rack was, by itself, a difficult and tiring job.

Not all of the hay would fit into the haymow so the rest was stacked into giant heaps out in the hay field. These had to be in accessible places for the farmer to collect feed for his animals during the winter. Henry worked hard at a young age to accomplish this.

We are told that Henry was not only a hard worker, but very resourceful. He had a vision for the future and was smart about making deals. He asked for a sow pig from a litter of pigs that Mr. Schooley owned for his pay for working Schooley's hay. Mr. Schooley agreed. Perhaps feed was scarce and Henry didn't have much money with which to buy it. Amazingly, Henry claimed he raised the sow on dishwater!!

The sow grew up, was bred, and had babies. Henry had his dad sell the pigs and he bought a heifer calf with his money. The heifer raised several calves and soon he owned a small herd of cattle. As his herd grew so did the credibility of Henry Wilson.

Henry Wilson later became the owner of the Dewy Dam Ranch south of Highmore, and achieved a reputation throughout central South Dakota as a very successful rancher in the 1940s and 50s.

SIXTEEN

Feeding the Family

PLANNING WAS important when there were so many mouths to feed. Charlie and Anna wanted the family to be healthy and always have enough food. Of course Anna preserved some food from the summer garden by canning. They also ordered several large crates of raisins, dried peaches, and other groceries from Sears and Roebuck every fall following their harvest.

Anna baked bread every other day. She baked delicious cinnamon rolls and made buns quite often. Anna also made pancakes nearly every day for breakfast. For a family their size, one can understand the need for a large supply of flour, and for it to last through the winter.

When they received word that the food they ordered had arrived at the train depot in Kimball, Charlie made a plan to bring the food home. He loaded up the wagon with grain to sell in Kimball. Then he purchased coal to bring home, along with the food from Sears for use through the long, cold winter months.

Often when Charlie went to collect the supplies for winter, the weather was already quite cold. He wore his long fur coat made from a buffalo hide, and walked beside the wagon with the horses to keep warm. The total distance to Kimball and home again was thirty-two miles. He left very early in the morning, and didn't get home until late at night.

There was great anticipation for Charlie to arrive home with the winter supplies. The children listened intently through the darkness of late afternoon or early evening for the rumble of the wagon and the clank of the horses' harnesses. The youngsters looked out the windows, or sometimes went outside and peered into the darkness, being very quiet so as to hear the horses a little ways down the road. If the dog barked, that might mean their dad was very near, which was another cue to run outside and listen.

This air of expectancy continued until he finally arrived home with all the supplies and special goodies, then there was great exuberance! The children were all talking and yelling at the same time. They wanted to see everything Charlie hauled home. He always brought special treats for the children. They all grouped around him in great expectation. So much excitement! It was almost like Christmas! This was one of Kate's favorite childhood memories.

When the excitement died down a bit, everyone helped unload and distribute the supplies for storage. This usually included twelve large 50-lb. sacks of flour for use over the next few months. Charlie stacked these in the closet of the bedroom Kate shared with Mary and Charlotte. The girls had no place to hang their dresses until some of the flour had been used. They were okay with that. Kate said they never thought of complaining about it. They happily found other places to put their clothes.

Other supplies might include dried fruit and vegetables to use in baking, and perhaps several yards of fabric to sew into dresses for the girls, and various pieces of clothing for the boys.

The surprises for Christmas gifts might also have been ordered so Charlie and Anna were careful to only distribute the sweet treats and school supplies for the present. It was difficult to hide some items because all the children were grouped around with great anticipation and lots of excited yelling and laughter.

The Unforgettable Storm of 1924

KATE'S ACCOUNT of the storm:

"It was late afternoon on that fateful day in 1924. My brother, Ira, and I were getting the cows into the corral for it was getting along to milking time. Suddenly it became much darker and we noticed an ominous, almost treacherous-looking brown-grey cloud rolling in from the southwest. It was truly rolling and pitching and appeared to be dangerous. My brother said, 'Let's let the cows go back to the pasture.' He seemed to realize they'd be better off there than in the barn, so we drove them back in that direction. We settled ourselves in the barn thinking it would blow over quickly but when it hit we decided differently so headed for the house. In route there we sought rest and shelter east of the chicken house but decided it wouldn't be shelter for long so headed to the house and made it there, and soon the chicken house blew away. Mom and four younger kids were there in the house and glad to see us come in. The big picture window on the north side of the front room was heaving in and out. Ira and I took pillows to hold against it hoping to save it but it blew in anyway. It blew us across the room and blew out the south window and sucked everything moveable on the wall from that room except the piano that set in the northwest corner of the room. Ira and I went into

the kitchen. Anna sent the younger kids to a protected bedroom and told them to stay there. We again tried to save the north window in the kitchen. We had better prospects there since the window was divided into smaller panes. The wind blew and raged and the rain poured down in torrents. It seemed as though it would never quit. We didn't know where our dad was farming.

The ceiling was now heaving up and down and we all wondered if the house would remain standing and if we would survive the storm. The storm kept on for an hour or more. When it did finally die down we went outside and found the chicken house completely gone. The garden and some crops were swept clean. As we were at the window we saw our dad crawling across the yard in the wind and the rain. He had started home on his little tractor but had left it and crawled home in the ditch beside the road. When Ira saw him he impulsively decided to go out and help his dad get into the house. He went out the east door and was promptly blown off the porch. My dad had to go rescue him and later he scolded him for leaving the house. Of course, instinctively Ira wanted to help his dad and forgot how deadly the storm was. My dad was badly beaten up by the wind and the rain but we were so glad to see him home safe and sound. The storm covered hundreds of miles and blew some houses down and many, many barns and windmills. Some churches were destroyed and some lives were lost. We, who lived through the storm, have vivid memories of the long, treacherous, continuous tornado of 1924."

Kate Wilson Gunderson Larsen

Kate Enters High School

CHARLIE TOLD Kate for many years that he wanted her to become a teacher. He would often say, "You'll make a great teacher, Duck." She never knew why he called her "Duck" but she agreed with her father about being a teacher and hoped that someday she would fulfill that dream.

Charlie wanted all his children to be educated. He was an avid reader, and the only farmer in his neighborhood in the early 1900s who subscribed to a daily newspaper. He was interested in national news and reading about events outside the local area. With a big family to care for Charlie had very little leisure time, but reading the daily paper was important to him. He also enjoyed reading books and poetry. He involved the family in social events in the community and wanted them to have insight and knowledge about a variety of professions and skills. He encouraged them to reach for opportunities outside of their comfort zones.

Charlie had not mentioned to Kate that he was searching for a place she could receive specialized teacher training while attending high school. He had read in the daily paper about such schools and this led him to more sources of information. His research indicated that students who attended high school at a "normal" school could be certified for a teaching certificate, which allowed them to teach grades 1-8 in rural schools in South Dakota. With two years of college, majoring in education, that student then became eligible to receive a State Teaching Certificate, and they could teach elementary grades anywhere in South Dakota. Later, "normal" schools eliminated their high school programs and became four-year colleges that offered degrees in education as well as most other professions.

For several years Charlie had pondered the possibility of sending Kate to high school at a "normal" school after she completed eighth grade. After much soul-searching, he decided she would attend high school on the campus of Southern State Normal, a teacher's college in Springfield, SD. When he presented his plan to Kate, she enthusiastically agreed.

In 1922, when Kate was 13 years old and had completed eight years of grade school, Charlie took her to Springfield, more than one hundred miles from the family home in Gann Valley. She would board at the college dormitory on campus. In her words, she was "very green" about being away from home. She had stayed overnight with neighbor friends previously, or with relatives with her mother, but she had never stayed by herself anywhere for an extended amount of time. The only time she would return home during the school term would be Christmas vacation. She had a lot to learn—and not all of it from a book.

On the designated day, Charlie and Kate rose very early. They loaded her suitcase and a lunch, knowing it would probably be late in the day when they arrived. Kate wondered why her mother did not even get out of bed to see her off and tell her goodbye. Strangely, her dad didn't offer any explanation, and she didn't ask. Perhaps her mother did not agree with her dad about sending her off to school? She later theorized her mother might have thought Kate had all the education she needed to become a wife and mother. Anna, being from the "old country," may have thought that what a girl did when she grew up was get married and have babies. Kate had already been experiencing doubts about leaving home for her education, and this odd behavior from her mother was not exactly a confidence-builder. However, her dad was determined to carry out the plan and they proceeded to Springfield.

There was an empty feeling in the pit of her stomach as she faced the unknown. She worried about missing her siblings, and wondered if she could come home if she didn't like Springfield. She thought of telling her dad she had changed her mind, but quickly ruled that out. It was too late to change. She just had to make the best of her situation. After all, "How bad could it be?"

They were traveling in a Model T Roadster on a graveled road. The day was cool and windy. The wind swirled around the car causing clouds of dirt from the bumpy road to rise up around them and quietly sift into the car as they traveled. Kate felt gloomy. Clouds of doubt weighed down on her and the sky mirrored her mood. Hours passed with very little conversation between the two of them.

It began to rain about halfway into the trip. The windows of the car were made from Isinglass, so at least something shielded them from the rain. It seemed they would never get to Springfield. Kate became increasingly uncomfortable. It was dusk when they arrived. Thankfully, they had driven out of the rain and the evening was shaping up to be peaceful and quiet.

Springfield was a quiet little town with a main street only about a block long. It seemed deserted. Most of the businesses had closed for the day. Charlie didn't know where to go first, so he asked a gentleman walking down the street where the president of the college could be found. The man was the only person on the street but was friendly and directed them to the residence of the college president, whom he referred to as President Lawrence.

Charlie and Kate found the Lawrence residence and approached the large outdoor porch that extended around two sides. Green shrubs surrounded the neatly painted house. It looked warm and inviting. They walked up the steps with great hesitation, not knowing who or what to expect. Charlie looked at Kate, who was feeling anxious and frightened. He reached for her hand and clasped it firmly to calm her.

They were pleasantly surprised, and relieved, to see a friendly middle-aged man who greeted them warmly and asked how he could help them. Charlie identified himself, and then introduced Kate, whom he explained he wanted to enroll in the school. The man at the door introduced himself as President Lawrence and invited them into the house. His wife welcomed them graciously, insisting she would prepare dinner for them since they had traveled all day. She also insisted that they would be overnight guests; Charlie could leave the next day, but not without proper rest!

Over dinner, Charlie told President Lawrence about himself and his family in Gann Valley. He expressed his strong belief that his daughter showed great promise to educate children. "I think she will make a great teacher," he said, "and I want her to have this opportunity for good quality teacher training."

President Lawrence informed them that school had already been in session for two weeks. He asked Kate if she thought she could make up that time. She nodded and answered that she could handle it. President Lawrence then assured Charlie he would take Kate over to the school the next morning to see that she was registered properly, and Charlie could go on home. President Lawrence and his wife promised to take good care of Kate.

The next morning, after her father left, Kate experienced moments of terror, wishing she could go back home. She was already homesick. She felt so alone. President Lawrence was very fatherly and comforting. He assured her she would soon feel comfortable, and told her to come by his office if she had questions.

As he had promised, he got Kate registered and walked her to her first class. She trembled as she entered a classroom full of faces she had never seen before. She wondered, "What will happen next? Where will I go for my next class?"

She was overwhelmed by the size of the buildings and the number of classrooms. The other students were already familiar with the campus and each other. With no school orientation Kate had no idea where to find the room for her next class. At home there was only one room in the whole school; this arrangement was so confusing. She didn't know anybody, so who could she ask? She didn't know where to turn and was paralyzed with fear. If only she could magically disappear!

Then a bell rang, doors opened, and students filed out into the hallway. They all seemed to be going somewhere and seemed to know their destination. Everyone was talking and laughing. No one paid any attention to Kate as they hurried to their next class. Kate knew she was supposed to go to a different room but had no idea where it was. The hallway became quiet as the students entered other rooms. Looking for Room 207, she was unaware that the "2" meant second floor. Hesitant to even open a classroom door, much less enter—especially since another session had started —she was frozen with fear. She again contemplated going home but quickly ruled that out when she pictured Charlie's disappointment. She couldn't bear to think about that. "I can't disappoint my dad! I can't. I *must* figure this out." How she yearned to see her dad and talk with him.

Kate studied her registration cards again and desperately tried to analyze her location. She couldn't sit in the hallway forever. She would have to enter a classroom and just endure the humiliation that would surely take place. Facing the door of a classroom her hands shook as she reached for the doorknob. She opened the door a little—not all the way—and the room grew deathly silent as she peeked in.

The instructor asked, "What do you need, Miss uh ... what is your name?"

In a weak voice, she replied, "Wilson. Kathryn Wilson. I am

looking for my algebra class." The students snickered and laughed. The professor asked to see her registration cards and then sternly ordered a young man to "please assist Miss Wilson in finding the proper classroom."

This painful experience took place several times before Kate figured out the locations of her daily classes.

Kate's new environment was very formal and proper; it took time for her to acclimate and learn how to navigate the formalities of this new campus life. And she did because she was determined to "make it work," no matter the cost.

Kate's experiences in the dormitory were not helpful either. She roomed with two older girls who attended college classes. They made no attempt to connect with her socially. They weren't mean to her; they just ignored her. This deprived Kate of the opportunity to develop a close and meaningful friendship with another girl her age—someone with whom she could share her experiences in the classroom, or just her daily life. She had no female figure to turn to with her problems, or for comfort when she was lonely or unsure how to handle certain social situations.

Kate had to learn a special protocol for the dining room. Students congregated in an outer room awaiting a bell to a signal it was time to enter the dining room. Everyone was assigned to a table and they were to stand behind their chair until the bell sounded again. This was the signal for a mealtime prayer. When the bell sounded a third time, they were permitted to sit down. Each student was expected to take a turn as the server at their table, which meant they were to dish the food onto the plate for each individual seated there. Kate was terrified! She had never done that and thought how terrible it would be if she spilled hot food on someone, or if she dropped something on the floor. The supervisors seemed to expect perfection and were stern and impatient.

She did not know all the fine manners required to eat "properly." She was reprimanded for not holding her fork correctly, and felt constantly critiqued by other students and the dining room supervisors. It was humiliating to be scolded by the supervisors for making a mistake. The other students whispered and laughed among themselves. She was so nervous she thought she might faint while learning the protocol for serving. With practice, however, she became more comfortable with those responsibilities.

No one was allowed to leave the dining room until the last bell sounded. The whole experience was very organized and regimented. Eventually she became so accustomed to eating in this manner she could hardly remember what it was like to eat with the family at home.

Kate's first year in Springfield was stressful and challenging. How she longed to go home and be with her family again. Every Tuesday she received a letter from Charlie telling her to stay strong and keep a "stiff upper lip." He kept telling her it would get better, encouraging her to "stay in the buggy." Somehow he surmised how difficult it was for her and tried his best to encourage and support her, especially since she didn't seem to have her mother's support.

Kate knew how disappointed her dad would be if she quit school and returned home. He believed in her so much that, in spite of her loneliness, she couldn't let him down. She learned to take one day at a time, and found she could excel in her academics, despite her other challenges. In addition to academic skills, she was learning to be resourceful, an independent thinker, and a decision maker. She became a survivor!

Years later, Kate gave her dad a lot of credit for helping her become a strong, competent, and resourceful woman. She admired her father for promoting the rights of women as she and her sisters grew up. And he always spoke with great respect and admiration for her mother, Anna.

After a summer at home, Kate was looking forward to tenth grade at Springfield. She now shared her father's dream. Perhaps she now owned the dream herself—to complete her education. She was happy to return and ready for new challenges.

Kate pleaded with Charlie to allow her to take at least one semester of beginning piano as she began tenth grade. It would be a hardship for her dad to pay the extra money for lessons, and though he couldn't afford to pay for many, she learned the necessary fundamentals. She practiced as many hours as she could squeeze into her day, looking for unscheduled slots in the practice rooms. So thrilled to at last be able to take lessons, she found practice wasn't dull at all. Kate progressed quickly. Her frustration of watching the neighbor girls play piano at home, and her aching to take the lessons she knew were out of reach then, were dispelled by this opportunity of a lifetime.

Kate struggled with one major problem in her second year of high school. There were times when she was in class and everything seemed normal, but then she would suddenly "wake up" and find she had been sleeping. She didn't know how or why she had fallen asleep but she found herself all alone in the classroom. These strange episodes only happened occasionally, but she was in shock each time. She didn't have any warning prior to an episode. There was never any change in her physical feelings. She didn't speak to anyone—a teacher, a doctor, or a nurse—about it. None of the teachers ever suggested she should see a doctor. She never understood why this happened but it frightened her, and of course contributed to her already-existing feelings of insecurity. She felt embarrassed and ashamed but didn't know what to do about it. In fact, she did nothing, and neither did anyone else. Eventually, to her relief, it just stopped happening. She never discovered what had caused it. These strange episodes had been a big worry to Kate and she was grateful when they stopped. When she was much older she thought maybe she had experienced seizures, but that was only her own diagnosis.

I have read that when this strange phenomena occurs to a young girl it is sometimes associated with hormonal imbalance, or changes taking place in their bodies. Kate eventually grew out of these unusual happenings and never experienced them again. She enjoyed outstandingly good health until she was 90 years old and often expressed gratitude for that blessing.

Kate found some good friends her second year at school. With other girls she sometimes hiked down to the Missouri River, which was only about a mile from Springfield. The river marked the border between South Dakota and Nebraska. There was a ferry that ran regularly from the South Dakota side to the Nebraska side. The girls loved to ride on the ferry and the gentleman who ran it would let them ride free if he didn't have many customers at that time. Sometimes they would go back and forth several times a day. They loved to brag about how many times they traveled to Nebraska on a given afternoon to see their friends.

Weekends were lonely for Kate because most of the students at Springfield Normal came from homes in the area so they went home then. President and Mrs. Lawrence turned out to be great friends to Kate. They seemed to like her and tried to make her life more bearable. She had fond memories of her times with them. Occasionally Mrs. Lawrence would entertain the faculty or a local ladies group. She invited Kathryn (the name she gave herself and wished to be called) to come to the Lawrence home and help her. Kate polished silverware, set tables, dished up desserts, etc., and after the guests left, helped by washing dishes and putting them away.

While they were doing these boring tasks together, she visited with Mrs. Lawrence, who often talked about her sons. One of the Lawrence boys attended college at Springfield while Kate was there. Kate spoke about how kind he was, and that even though he seemed a lot older than she was, he always greeted her respectfully. Mrs. Lawrence told Kate that when her other son Ernest came home from college in the East, she would be invited to dinner so she could meet him.

True to her word, Mrs. Lawrence really did invite Kate to the house for dinner to meet Ernest, the oldest Lawrence brother. Kate was impressed with how the family made her feel comfortable and important in their presence. They centered their conversation around Kate and her family.

Ernest Lawrence was the nuclear physicist who invented the cyclotron—the original atom smasher—for which he received the Nobel Prize for Physics in 1939. He was the first professor from a public university and the first native of South Dakota to win the prize. His parents, Carl and Gunda Lawrence, both offspring of Norwegian immigrants, met while teaching at the high school in Canton, SD, where Carl was also the superintendent of schools. Ernest was born in 1901. Gunda was quoted as saying that Ernest was "born grown up." Ernest received a B.S. Degree in chemistry in 1922 from the University of South Dakota. He received an M.A. in physics from the University of Minnesota in 1923 and went on to Yale University where he earned his Ph.D. in physics in 1925. (Source: *Science Beat*, October 1, 2001 by Lynn Yarris)

Kate completed two years of education at Springfield Normal. When she was ready for her third year Charlie experienced difficult economic times. He could not afford to pay tuition for her and she had to attend high school in Kimball, SD. Charlie had arranged a place for her to stay with a family where she could work for her board and room while she attended school. He didn't want her to quit and this was a way she could continue her education. Kate was extremely disappointed because now she really loved school in Springfield. She understood the financial situation, however, and was still determined to finish her high school education.

Kate and friends at Springfield 1924

She felt the quality of her education at Springfield was the best anywhere and regretted not being able to finish high school there. Kate always felt blessed for the opportunity to attend school at Southern for two years and recognized her experiences there as a solid foundation for her future. Her time there definitely helped her develop inner strength, self-confidence, and leadership qualities which she found useful as she matured.

Kate completed her eleventh year of school in Kimball. She

lived with and worked for a local family to pay for her room and board. Her duties included the household chores often neglected by the lady of the house. The daily chores included taking the children out for a walk and fully caring for them in the evening hours until their bedtime. The family seldom allowed her to take time off for extra-curricular school functions and were not especially warm or friendly to her at any time. She was treated like a paid household servant. Though the year was not entirely pleasant, she endured, and completed her junior year. She expected to return the next year.

The summer before Kate was to be a senior in high school, a gentleman came to the Wilson farm one day to speak with Charlie. The man had heard Charlie's daughter might work for room and board while attending high school. He explained that because his wife had been hospitalized for over a month due to a serious illness, they would need help in their home while her health improved. He asked if Kate would consider employment with them while attending school in Gann Valley. Kate was eager to take the job. Her dad said it was her choice, so she chose to stay with the Del Hubbard family in Gann Valley, and work for her room and board while she was a senior in high school.

The Hubbards were very kind to Kate. They wanted her senior year to be one to remember and, even though she was working for her room and board, they encouraged her to participate in all the school activities. It was quite different from the situation in Kimball and Kate found her year very enjoyable. She earned excellent grades and had many opportunities to participate in activities in Gann Valley. She was in declamation, music, and had a major role in an operetta that was performed by the junior and senior classes.

Kate graduated from Gann Valley High School in 1926 with seven other class members. The senior class included Peggy Payne, Bill Stephans, Frank Wulff, Edna Thompson, Anna Marshall, Bertha Swartout, Ella Johnson, and Kate. The girls in her class decided to design and sew special dresses for themselves to wear for graduation. There were many all-girl meetings to plan the strategy for designing their dresses. How proud she felt as she crossed the stage to receive her high school diploma in her own specially designed dress.

Kate had many fond memories of her senior year at Gann Valley High School. This was a year she matured and gained poise and self-confidence as she provided class leadership. She was facing a new world filled with possibilities, challenges, and responsibilities and felt prepared and fully capable of making wise choices and handling new and exciting opportunities. She was ready to step into her future.

The University of South Dakota at Springfield was a state-supported university in Springfield, SD that was founded in 1881 and closed in 1984. It started as Southern State Normal School and became Southern State Teachers College in 1947, Southern State College in 1964, and finally the University of South Dakota at Springfield in 1971. The campus is now home to Mike Durfee State Prison, which is named for a star athlete and teacher at the school.

(Content is available under CC BY-SA 3.0)

DON'T QUIT

When things go wrong as they sometimes will,
When the road you're trudging seems all up hill,
And you want to smile, but you have to sigh,
When the funds are low and the debts are high
When care is pressing you down a bit,
Rest, if you must but don't you quit.

Life is queer with its twists and turns,
As everyone of us sometimes learns,
And many a failure turns about
When he might have won had he stuck it out;
Don't give up though the pace seems slow—
You may succeed with another blow,
Success is failure turned inside out—
The silver tint of the clouds of doubt,
And you never can tell how close you are,
It may be near when it seems so far;
So stick to the fight when you're hardest hit—
It's when things seem worst that you must not quit.

Edgar Albert Guest

NINETEEN

Look Out World!

WHEN KATE GRADUATED from high school in 1926, South Dakota allowed a high school graduate to teach school, under certain conditions. Students who had received a high school diploma, then attended one term of summer school studying qualifying subjects, and who then passed a state exam could be certified to teach grades one through eight. Kate still possessed a strong desire to become a teacher so she decided to return to Springfield for summer school.

At the end of the summer term, students were required to write an exam to certify their readiness to teach. Kate wrote her exam at Gann Valley in the office of the Buffalo County School Superintendent. She passed with flying colors and was awarded her teaching certificate; she could now teach elementary grades in South Dakota.

Kate was hired to teach in a school in Buffalo County. There were fifteen students attending grades 1-8. This school was an enormous challenge, even for an experienced teacher. The only help available to Kate would be the County Superintendent Mrs. Fite who visited each of the rural schools twice a year to observe the teacher and check the school conditions. After this visit she would tell each teacher what she observed, and suggest improvements. She gave Kate credit for doing a good job. Many years later, when reflecting on that year, Kate expressed that she was awfully young, at age 18, to take on this challenge. She thought that she probably didn't teach much to those students, and that she was the one who really got an education.

Since Kate didn't live near that school, she boarded with one of the school patrons whose children attended there. She agreed to pay them a certain amount of money to eat the evening meal daily and stay overnight four nights each week. This arrangement usually benefitted the teacher and also allowed the family to make a little extra income. In her case, this family agreed to also provide transportation for her in bad weather.

Kate's duties included keeping the schoolhouse clean and knowing how to bank a fire in the stove so the coals would stay hot enough for the fire to ignite again the next morning when she fed it more fuel. If this wasn't done, it would take a long time to get a good fire going again and heat the school to a comfortable temperature.

The biggest challenge was to actually educate the children in each class. Kate found this both an opportunity and a trial, and said she often regretted not finding enough hours in the day to reach each child. Even when she taught in a smaller school, she never felt satisfied that she had reached each child daily in the most effective way.

Kate recalled a special event at the home of the Viereck family, whose children attended her school. They had invited her to stay overnight, and that evening hosted a party, inviting several young people from the neighborhood. A big Edison Victrola phonograph played records all evening, and everyone danced in the parlor. A young man by the name of Bill Larsen asked Kate to dance several times. This new acquaintance blossomed into a romance for a short time.

Kate didn't remember what her salary was for her first teaching job but did remember thinking she was becoming wealthy. Dad Wilson told her that when she started teaching, he expected her to contribute financially to educate her younger sisters. She agreed and helped support each of them not only financially, but also in many other ways. The younger ones relied on Kate for support emotionally, and for advice in many situations.

In order to keep her teaching certificate current, Kate had to continue attending summer school. After her first year teaching, she chose to attend classes at Black Hills Normal in Spearfish, SD. Ruth Peterson, a young woman from Wessington Springs who also needed to keep her certificate current, went with her. The women roomed together at the dormitory on campus and did a lot of their studying together. They also had time to enjoy a social life on and off campus. They hiked in the hills for exercise and fun.

Kate in Spearfish SD, 1928.

One day some young men from Kimball were driving around Spearfish and recognized Kate as she and Ruth were walking downtown. Kate vaguely remembered meeting the young man from Kimball who was driving the car. The girls accepted a ride to the campus. They all agreed to take a drive through the Black Hills on the weekend and get better acquainted. These four spent a lot of time together touring the hills, hiking, and having picnics on the weekends. Kate had good memories of that summer.

For her second year of teaching Kate signed a contract for a school in Jerauld County. It was close to the home of her brother Henry and his wife, Jennie. Henry had recently married Jennie Miles from Gann Valley and they were renting a farm near Kate's new school. She conveniently boarded at their home that year.

Kate had been acquainted with Jennie, but that year the two became very close friends. Jennie came from a light-hearted family that appreciated humor. Kate loved living with Jennie and Henry and recalled many times when they all laughed at life. Jennie never took any situation too seriously. Many years later she and Kate laughed about the times they had conspired to play jokes on Henry.

TWENTY

Romance and Marriage

EVEN THOUGH KATE WAS TEACHING, she still continued to spend many weekends at the Wilson home with her family. The younger siblings had house parties to which they invited many friends from the surrounding area. On one such occasion, the girls informed Kate they had heard about a young man from Wessington Springs who worked with his brothers on their ranch near Gann Valley. They described him as very handsome, and according to their "sources" he was not dating anyone. The sisters thought they should invite him to their party to get acquainted. Kate was agreeable so the sisters contacted their "sources" to pass on the invitation.

The night of the party the Wilson girls were excited about meeting this young, handsome, eligible bachelor. They didn't know much about him except he had recently returned from California and was working with his brothers on the Gunderson Ranch, not far away. When almost everyone had arrived and they thought the handsome bachelor might not be coming, one of the other neighbor boys arrived, and with him the new young man, Jim. He was just as handsome as they had been told and they couldn't wait to dance with him. He asked Kate to dance once and then retreated to the kitchen, where Charlie was sitting. He visited with Charlie the rest of the evening and never danced another dance.

The girls were disappointed and thought they would never see him again.

Charlie, however, was highly impressed.

And Kate's sisters were wrong. Jim returned to ask Kate to go out with him. A romance blossomed between Kate and the handsome bachelor, as the rest of the girls "oohed and aahd" each time they saw him.

In the spring of 1929 Jim and Kate became engaged and were married October 29, 1929. A very small wedding was held in Wessington Springs, with Pastor Parnell Nelson—the pastor of the Lutheran church Jim attended—officiating. Jim's brother, Carl Gunderson, was his best man, and Carl's girlfriend and future wife, Ruth Peterson, was bridesmaid for Kate. There were no guests and, unfortunately, no traditional wedding photographs of the couple to mark their wedding day.

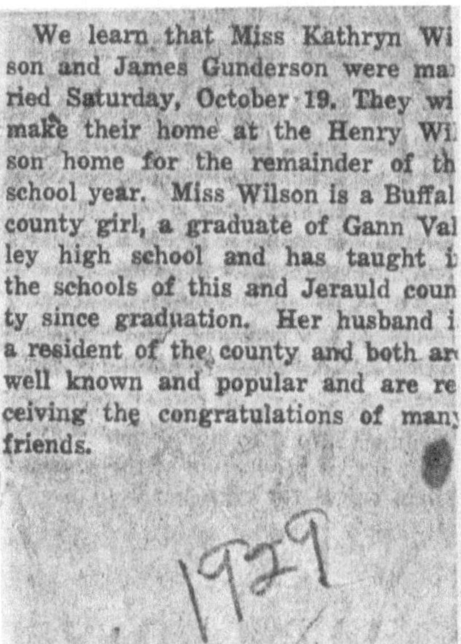

We learn that Miss Kathryn Wilson and James Gunderson were married Saturday, October 19. They will make their home at the Henry Wilson home for the remainder of the school year. Miss Wilson is a Buffalo county girl, a graduate of Gann Valley high school and has taught in the schools of this and Jerauld county since graduation. Her husband is a resident of the county and both are well known and popular and are receiving the congratulations of many friends.

Jim had a brand new Ford roadster. He and Kate decided to forego a honeymoon and instead pay for the car. Money was in short supply for both. For a few months—until they were able to rent a small farm in Jerauld County—the newlyweds lived with Kate's brother and his wife, Henry and Jennie Wilson.

When the school term ended, Kate decided not to teach the following year. She wanted to stay home and be a homemaker. That summer she planted a garden and canned lots of vegetables. She enjoyed keeping house and cooking. Jim had acquired 5 or 6 cows and some chickens and was setting up to be a farmer. Their future looked good.

Kate and Jim had settled nicely into a routine. Jim eventually acquired a team of horses to for farming and was able to work a deal with some neighbors to use some of their machinery temporarily, for plowing and planting.

The next year Kate became pregnant; the baby was expected to arrive in May. Kate made arrangements to deliver at the home of

Ed and Ida Renando (Ida was Jim's sister), who lived in a small Norwegian community about 12 miles southwest of Wessington Springs. Dr. Jenkinson, the local doctor, was present for the delivery. He was more than a little apprehensive about delivering the baby so far out in the country. There was no running water or electricity. Kate was in labor for longer than he considered normal—it was nearly twenty-four hours before Merrill James was born on May 12, 1931. He weighed 8 lbs., 8 oz., and the doctor announced he was perfectly normal.

Jim went out to report to the world that he was now a father, and the baby was a boy. When he told Grandma Gunderson—his Norwegian mother who was originally from Norway—she said, "You named him WHAT?? Merrill! What kind of name is that? Why didn't you name him something easy, like Yimmy Herman?" That was the name she had given Jim. He found her so amusing that he related this story for many years, with hearty laughter. Since Jim was a very quiet man we know he found this story very humorous.

Merrill was a fussy baby for a few months. Kate thought he suffered from colic, so at first caring for him was challenging, but each day he seemed to improve until he became a happy, healthy baby.

TWENTY-ONE

The Dirty Thirties

IN 1931 THE depression and severe drought made for a very poor year for farmers in South Dakota, and in many other states. The grain that Jim planted in the spring came up and looked like a beautiful crop, until it froze. He planted the grain a second time, sure it would be fine. Not so; it froze again. Jim and other farmers were devastated. Next, hot winds arrived and continued throughout the growing season. There was no rain. The hot winds literally cooked the corn crop on the stalks. There was no rain.

Kate's dad Charlie brought his tractor and binder to Kate and Jim's farm at harvest time to help Jim cut his burning corn to use as fodder to feed his animals. Emil, one of Kate's younger brothers, came along to help with the cutting. While riding the binder he somehow lost his balance and fell into the cutting mechanism below him. He was badly injured. They took him to a town doctor who made many stitches on Emil's face, hands, and arms. Thankfully, he recovered well.

It seemed everything farmers tried that year ended badly. If they didn't have bad luck they had no luck at all. Not because they were doing things wrong but because the weather was terribly dry. The winds blew every day, hot and intense. Additionally, the economic depression was having a terrible effect on people all over the United States. Many farms were sold because the owners didn't have enough money to pay their property taxes. These folks had to find a different place to live. Conditions became worse instead of improving. It was a very dark time in history, and Kate and Jim were in the middle of it.

Since things were not going well on the rented farm, Jim decided they should move to the Gunderson homestead, not far away. Jim's brother Carl had been living there, so he moved to another place. This was the farm where Jim and Carl had grown up, along with their siblings Gus, Selmer, "Cap," Dora, and Ida.

Kate raised chickens and Jim was milking cows so they had cream and eggs to sell for groceries and gas. Kate couldn't imagine how the cows could give any milk since there was so little grass available for grazing. There was still no rain—weeds didn't even grow. Nobody had any crops, anywhere. Kate said there was barely enough income to buy groceries but she never thought of not including a can of Prince Albert tobacco and cigarette papers for Jim. The tobacco cost a quarter but it was a high priority!

It was the "dirty thirties" and nobody had money for entertainment; there was barely enough money for food. There were few opportunities for employment besides farming, and that was anything but prosperous. Life was depressing for everybody.

Quite a few young people lived in the community around the Gunderson place. Kate felt if the community youth gathered for some games and fellowship it might make their circumstances more bearable. She started by inviting everyone to the Gunderson home and suggested they keep meeting each week. All agreed. They usually sang some of their favorite songs and then played games and had a lunch. There were 15-18 young people and they looked forward to the fun and fellowship.

In the summer the guys put together a couple of baseball teams and had a game every week. The women and kids were spectators and chose a team to cheer for. It was a good way for families to get together. Sometimes they had a picnic the day of the game.

Kate was a good organizer and felt these activities created an opportunity for camaraderie and close friendships. They could at least all be miserable together instead of suffering alone. A community Sunday School was started in the Happy Hill schoolhouse, which was located about a mile from Jim and Kate. Kate became the Sunday School teacher for the youth. She was always positive, enthusiastic, and a willing volunteer who wanted to be involved with the young people around her. The Sunday School endured and continued well into the next decade.

Kate was amazed at the talented and intelligent people in the community around her. She found them to be very social and cooperative. A few years earlier the community had started a series of evening programs at the school that they called the Literary Society. She eagerly participated in these programs, which consisted of a variety of activities for all age groups such as debates, plays, and musical performances. Everyone was interested in being involved and each program was well attended. People brought cookies or cake for lunch, and they always served coffee. Folks had found a way to make life a little more bearable in hard times. These activities gave them a reason to smile. They also bonded in friendship so they became like one big family.

With dust storms and the economic depression, no one had money, and the value of money and property taxes was in question. Huge dust storms raged, crops failed, livestock starved, and times were hard—nearly impossible. In 1934 Gann Valley experienced heat that measured at 120° Fahrenheit!

In 1935 the Gunderson place, where Jim and Kate lived, was sold at auction for unpaid property taxes. Kate and Jim moved to what was known as the Crist place. It was in the same proximity and they still enjoyed the same neighbors. Merrill was almost four years old and they were expecting their second child.

Jim was working with the WPA (the Works Progress Administration), a program created during the Great Depression while Franklin Delano Roosevelt was president. The government paid a small wage to help people affected by the depression and drought while creating a work force to build and repair the infrastructure of the country. This provided jobs and income to mostly unskilled men, and carried out public works projects like the construction of public buildings and roads. Jim worked on roads, bridges, dugouts, dams, and other similar rural public projects. The men also planted shelter belts to prevent soil erosion. The government also provided certain food commodities for low-income families. It was definitely a win-win plan and breathed new life and hope into the country.

Jim and the other men rose early every day, hitched up their own teams of horses to wagons, and traveled to the location of their work. They faced all kinds of weather—cold, snow, sleet, rain, sunshine, and intense heat. There was plenty of all! Kate described the heat as relentless and the drought severe.

Jim kept milking cows and continued to plant his crops every year in an effort to keep his farming operation alive. They always hoped that "this year maybe it will be better." It was all in vain. The dust smothered everything and everybody. Fence lines were nearly covered by huge drifts of dust, like snowbanks. There were grasshoppers; so many grasshoppers that they nearly covered the ground. They ate every edible thing in sight and more. They sometimes ate the fence posts! During the dust storms the wind was intense for long periods of time. Dust blew around like snow in a blizzard. Some days it was dark all day long, making it difficult for farmers to care for their few surviving animals. Farm wives needed to light their lamps in the house in order to do their work. Kate remembered dipping dish towels in water and hanging them at the windows to keep some of the dust from getting into their house. This area was what became known as the "dust bowl." It would be years of barely surviving before things got better.

Well, babies continued to arrive in spite of the dust storms. Gayle Corrine was born to Jim and Kate Gunderson on November

23, 1935 at the Cowan Maternity Home in Wessington Springs, SD. She weighed in at 10 lbs.! She was a big girl! Kate reported that "she was healthy and happy and content with life most all the time, and Merrill was happy to entertain her when he was needed."

Kate's children Gayle and Merrill around 1938

Kate sometimes boarded teachers. A year or two after my birth (I am Gayle), Roberta Christensen taught at the Hall School, one mile south of our farm. She boarded with us, and she and Kate became close friends. Mid-year Roberta became seriously ill and sadly wasn't able to finish the school year. Kate completed the school term as the teacher. A sixteen-year-old neighbor girl became my baby sitter. By this time, Merrill was in first grade. Kate received $35 per month salary and paid the baby sitter $10 per month. When I was five years old my mother decided to send me to school because I would be six that November.

My parents neighbored with the Wenzels, who had a family of older girls. Mary Lou, the youngest of their girls, was an eighth grader at Hall School. She paid a lot of attention to me. I thought she was beautiful with her long blonde hair and beautiful blue eyes. When we walked to and from school each day I always walked with Mary Lou. I often saw her outside of school, too, because our parents were such good friends.

When my brother and I learned we would be moving to a different farm a long way off, I was worried and upset. What would I do without Mary Lou? She was like my big sister. My mother kept assuring me there would be some girls in my new school for me to like and that I shouldn't worry. Preparations continued for the move.

Jim and Kate with their children Merrill and Gayle around 1942

TWENTY-TWO

Moving Brings Big Changes

OUR FAMILY MOVED in March 1941 to a farm a few miles northwest of Wessington Springs. My brother and I would now attend the Eddy School, one mile from our new home. We would likely walk to school and home.

Soon after we moved in, my dad made contact with a gentleman who owned a number of Shetland ponies. He made a deal with that gentleman to take care of one pony—perhaps because the owner didn't have enough grassland to adequately feed all his ponies, and he really didn't want to sell them. Whatever the reason, we were surprised one day to see a truck drive into our farmyard containing a cute little orange-and-white spotted pony named Peaches. The driver unloaded the pony and drove away. Our dad said Merrill and I would ride Peaches to school. We were very excited, and Kate was pleased we had an opportunity to learn to ride horseback.

Having some riding experience would have been helpful before we began riding Peaches. Shetland ponies are smart and very perceptive about their handlers. On our first day riding her to Eddy School, we mounted—riding double—with Merrill in front holding the reins, and me behind him. We thought the pony would just start walking, and calmly and dutifully carry us to school. Peaches, however, immediately recognized us as beginners. She wasn't going anywhere without persuasion.

My dad said, "Well, I guess you'll need to kick her belly with your heels." Merrill kicked the little pony's tummy and nothing happened. He tried again and again, and several more times. Peaches just stood still and calmly looked around. My dad, being a little impatient, picked up a board and mildly whacked her from behind to encourage her. Peaches took a few reluctant steps and stopped. We repeated this process all the way down the driveway. When we got on the road Peaches started walking, slowly, but moving ahead. My dad thought everything was going well and went back to the house.

When we topped the first hill behind our house and got a short distance on the other side, Peaches decided this trip was not in her schedule for the day and she casually "dumped" us in the ditch with a clever little buck. She turned and looked at us a moment, threw her head in the air, and trotted back to the farm.

In March there can still be snow in the ditches, which was the case that day, so it cushioned our fall. We got up and brushed the snow off our clothes.

Merrill expressed his anger. "Doggone the son-of a gun," he repeated at least five or more times as he started back home. I followed, a long way behind him.

When we arrived home our dad met us with the pony, reins in hand, saying, "You gotta let this pony know who is boss." He put us on Peaches once again and took us out to the driveway, this time following us a little way up the hill. All seemed to be going well so he returned to the house. Peaches picked the same spot to "dump" us again and threw her head in the air as if to say, "So there! This is really fun!" She trotted back home, leaving us in the ditch, and Merrill forgot that he was taught not to swear. He came up with some new names to call Peaches. We returned home the second time and my dad said, "Okay, we'll try this one more time."

We got on Peaches, she proceeded up the hill, and "dumped" us a third time. She was having the time of her life! She had total control.

We had a family meeting in the house to decide what to do next. Kate tried to hide her amusement; she was not taking this very seriously. My dad was a little angry with her, and a little angry at the pony. Kate suggested that Jim take us to school in the car and maybe he should teach Merrill how to handle the pony before he assumed he would know what to do as the rider.

Clearly Jim had lost patience with the whole situation. He literally threw us in the car and drove us to school. He had a few choice words about Peaches, too. He made time later, however, to teach us some about riding and eventually we gained control over Peaches. She dutifully transported us to school each day and we became more skillful riders.

Two big events took place in our family that summer.

First, my dad decided he needed a tractor to do his farm work. I remember the day someone drove a little red "B" Farmall tractor into our yard. I was rather mystified about who was driving, and watched with great interest as it came closer to the house. The driver was my dad! When he stopped and got off the tractor, he had biggest grin on his face that I ever saw on him. We were all thrilled and happy for him, and the tractor made his life a lot easier. He wasn't going to get rid of his team of horses, but he wouldn't need to work them like he did before, so their life got a lot better too. He kept them and occasionally they were useful. He became more accustomed to using his tractor, however, and finally retired his horses out to pasture.

In the eyes of a child, a second great event happened when a truck with a pony in the back again arrived in our yard. The driver unloaded a beautiful little blue roan Shetland pony. My dad said I would be riding Bluebell to school next year. Merrill would ride Peaches. I was beyond thrilled! I would be a second grader, was going on seven years old, and I had my own pony to ride! By then, I was quite accustomed to riding Peaches and I knew the routine about putting on the bridle, how to make the ponies stop and go, and how to feed them. Bluebell fit me like a glove. She was very small and rather lean, with graceful slender little legs. I could easily crawl on her back without help. Peaches was a little larger and plumper. I would always love Peaches, but now I was in love with Bluebell, too.

Lots of kids rode ponies to school then and many schools had a little shack on the grounds to provide shelter for them during the day. The school we attended that year was the Beers school and there was a nice little barn on the yard. When we arrived at school we fed some hay to the horses and checked them a few times during the day. When school was dismissed we bridled up the ponies to go home.

Merrill said to me, "Okay, I will hold her while you get on. Make sure you have your hands gripping her mane. Now, put the reins in this hand and put your legs around her belly. Are you ready?"

"Yes," I replied.

"Are you sure?" he asked me again.

I assured him I was ready.

"Okay, hang on!" he ordered.

He let go of Bluebell, and she bolted as fast as her little legs would take her—with me on her back, my head down, fingers laced tightly in her mane, and my legs firmly clamped around her little belly. She ran the entire mile to our farm. We were just one speedy little unit, Bluebell and me. Down the hill we went, over the bridge, and up the hill on the other side. She never slowed down until she took the driveway on two legs and headed for the water tank. My dad, often telling this story through his laughter, said he thought he would have to fish me out of the water tank someday because Bluebell stopped the very instant her front hooves rested on the base of it. Thankfully, I never landed in the water tank, even though this process repeated itself every school day that year.

I have no recollection of much that happened that year of school except the rides I had on Bluebell. A neighbor girl became my horseback riding buddy for the next year. We rode all summer together, nearly every day, in our pastures and beyond. Sometimes we got as far as the Wessington Hills. When I was at home I spent my time with the ponies in the corral, just talking with them. I crawled on their backs, slid down their necks, crawled under their bellies and they just kept eating and watching me. They were always there for me.

Reflecting on riding around the country with my friend, I find myself wondering why my mother would allow me to be gone all afternoon without checking on me. There were no cell phones, so I was not able to check in and tell her my whereabouts. Kate seemed to have confidence in me and was always supportive of my riding; she never discouraged me. She often said, "I knew you would come home when you got hungry." She encouraged me to be independent and to explore safe places and didn't place limits on me. She trusted me to make wise choices on my own.

Then one day the man who had left the ponies with us came to get them. We had no idea he was coming so I wasn't prepared. As I looked on helplessly, I watched him load our ponies in his truck and drive away. I was absolutely heartbroken. It was as though someone took my sister or brother. My grief was indescribable. I cried for days. Kate tried to console me but no one could make me feel better. She explained what the situation was, and she wept with me. She was as sad as I over the loss of the ponies. She felt my grief and she lived it with me.

I will never forget the pain of the sudden loss of my best friends. Strangely, even though so many years have passed, I still get emotional as I share my memories of Peaches and Bluebell. They were my whole world at that time in my life, and I am still moved to tears, feeling that pain, even as I record this story so many years later. The ponies will remain among the most beautiful memories of my life.

Reflecting on my sadness, I remember how my mother held me when I cried, without telling me to "get over it." She patiently listened to me and allowed me to express my grief by yelling and sobbing; and when I was quieter we talked about the joy the ponies had brought to our family. She created other situations I could get involved in and other things to think about, but we talked about the ponies a lot. She helped me grieve my loss. She allowed me to work my way through it all without criticism or impatience. Thanks to my mother's love and patience, I slowly healed and moved on.

Jim and Gayle with Fritzie, our very best pony, about 1944

Within a year my uncle Henry Wilson found a great little pony for Merrill and me. His name was Fritz. He was larger than a Shetland pony but smaller than a horse. He was perfect for us and we grew to love him as much as the other ponies. He was part of the family until well after Merrill and I both graduated from high school. Fritz had a long history of being loved by many children.

TWENTY-THREE

Kate Teaches Again

WHEN I WAS GOING into third grade, the township school board came to call on my parents. They offered Kate a position teaching at the Beers School. Conditions for my parents had improved but they felt they still needed more money to make ends meet. They agreed that Kate should sign the contract to teach at the Beers school for the next term. Merrill and I would attend school there and commute with our mother. She needed to attend summer school classes again to renew her teaching certificate. This time she enrolled at the Free Methodist Jr. College in Wessington Springs.

At school we had a wonderful Christmas program that year. We sang lots of Christmas songs and had a school play. Some students sang solos and some did recitations. My mother had my dad come and help her string wire from one side of the school to the other in the front of the room so she could hang sheets for curtains. Then they sectioned off a small area on each side of the front curtains so we had a back stage. Kate played the piano to accompany us as we sang. She had prepared a school program unlike and better than most school programs the patrons were accustomed to attending.

One wintry afternoon after school Merrill and I were waiting in the car outside the school for Kate to finish her preparations for the next day. She came out the door, her arms loaded with books and papers she intended to check at home. After she locked the door she turned toward the car but slipped on some ice on the concrete entrance to the school. She fell, and all the papers went in different directions.

Merrill and I ran and collected the papers and took them to her but she wasn't able to get up. She knew she had broken her arm. We helped her to the car. She told Merrill he would have to drive. He had never driven the car. He was only allowed to start the motor, but he had never driven! He got behind the steering wheel with Kate seated in the middle, and me next to the window on the passenger side, all in the front seat. She would instruct Merrill on how to drive.

This was a 1935 V-8 Ford sedan with a stick shift—the only kind of transmission in existence at that time. In order to drive these cars one had to push a pedal on the floorboard, called the clutch, with the left foot and hold it down while shifting gears with the right hand, all while keeping the gas feed down slightly with the right foot, so the motor would not kill. The driver normally changed gears three times in a kind of rhythm that took a considerable amount of practice. If the driver didn't get it right the car lurched and made a terrible sound as the metal gears ground together; and then the motor died.

That fateful afternoon we lurched ahead repeatedly, gears grinding, as the motor killed over and over. Merrill struggled to work his hands and feet together in a manner that would keep the car moving forward to the road where he also had to make a turn. Kate fainted twice, falling over the gear shift. I was screaming and bawling—I was sure she had died.

Merrill yelled for me to "shut up." There was a lot going on and Merrill was extremely stressed!

Finally, Merrill got the car on the road and we slowly worked our way home. Thankfully, we only had a mile to go; but I have often thought my little Bluebell would have made the trip much faster.

When we arrived home my dad got in the driver's seat and instructed Merrill to take me into the house and find something to eat. Jim and Kate went into Wessington Springs to find the doctor to set and cast my mother's broken arm.

Merrill and I were relieved when our parents arrived home much later that evening. I was happy to see my mother had lived through her ordeal. I think I appreciated her more at that time than ever before … or perhaps ever again.

Kate was a strong, stalwart soul, and never felt sorry for herself. She made all the necessary adjustments to resume a normal life, both at home and at school. She taught herself how to use her left hand—even to write—and remained independent and self-suffi-cient. My dad taught my brother how to drive the car, and life was good again.

Reliving that incident makes me appreciate the invention of the cell phone, which most of us carry with us at all times nowadays. Access to a cell phone would certainly have made this situation a whole lot more manageable.

TWENTY-FOUR

Communication

THE CHARLIE WILSON family didn't have a telephone in their home when Kate was growing up, but Kate and Jim always had a phone in their home. During the "dirty thirties" Kate called the phone company to request they remove the phone since she and Jim could not pay for the service. The company told her to keep the phone and maybe someday they would be able to pay the monthly fee. They kept the phone, and when times started to improve, Kate and Jim did resume monthly payments to the phone company. I seriously doubt any telephone company today would conduct their business in this manner.

The phones in those days were wooden boxes about 18" x 10," mounted on the wall high enough so the average adult could easily speak into the mouthpiece while standing. The bell-shaped receiver was attached to one side of the box with a cable 12"-18" long and the diameter of clothesline rope. It was bell-shaped for the person to put up to their ear so they could hear the voice of the caller. Often there was a step stool placed near the phone for children or short people to stand on.

Every residence was assigned a special ring. A small handle that rotated in a circular fashion was attached on the opposite side of the receiver. The caller used this handle to crank out the rings when making a call. If one wanted to call a neighbor whose ring was a long and three shorts they would crank the handle three quick successive short cranks (for long) and three short cranks with a second between them. The operator called from Central/Information once each day with the correct time and weather, or to alert us to emergencies. This was a common ring to all customers.

Before dial telephones, the caller reached the operator by cranking the handle on the side of the box on the wall. There was always an answer and one could ask most any question. When information was needed—such as the correct time, or someone's number, or help placing a call on a dial phone—the caller dialed "0."

I have childhood memories of calling Information for things other than the time of day. We felt comfortable asking questions about the weather, the cost of certain items, and for advice on our personal problems. It was like talking with our grandmother. The operators listened patiently and offered answers or possible solutions.

Time moved on and we children grew older. Telephone operators became more professional and were required to adhere to guidelines regarding privacy and confidentiality. Nevertheless, I have fond memories of the times when I felt free to share my personal problems with a voice on the telephone, without fear of repercussions.

We felt free to share our personal lives at that time, and I reflect—with a degree of sadness—how impersonal we have become, seemingly out of necessity and safety. There was a time when we were not fearful of reaching out to someone we didn't know, and did not need to fear that doing so could be detrimental to our physical health and/or our financial well-being. The voice from "Central/Information" seemed to have feelings like the rest of us, and an identity we could trust with our personal information.

There were usually 8-10 families on each rural phone line. All the neighbors could hear when someone was being called and they always knew *who* was being called. It was a common practice to "rubber," which meant that some of the neighbors listened in to the conversation when someone else was called. We all knew there were listeners on the line and as a result gossip spread like wildfire. Privacy was a non-issue in those days. We all knew what had happened in someone else's family well ahead of the time they informed us personally.

Kate lived long enough to own a cell phone and she was adept at using it. She didn't have internet on it but she found this technology fascinating and wanted to learn more. She was a quick learner. She also owned a computer for a few years. She had many friends on email and conversed with them often. When the computer failed we didn't replace it, and that is one of the things I most regret. I wish I would have had the foresight to introduce her to the internet and instruct her on how to find information on it before macular degeneration took her sight.

Country Peddler

MY DAD, Jim, had three older brothers in his family, one younger half-brother, and two half- sisters. They all lived on farms or ranches near Wessington Springs or Gann Valley. We only gathered with them for holidays or special occasions—except for Carl and Ruth, whom we saw more frequently.

Selmar—called Sam—one of Jim's older brothers, lived in Wessington Springs. Selmar never married. We thought he was pretty set in his ways as a bachelor. When he was older he shared his home with Grandma Gunderson, and cared for her until her death.

Gus and "Cap" Gunderson owned a cattle ranch together near Gann Valley, SD. They were popular ranchers, and well-known in the community for their storytelling and colorful conversation, which was often sprinkled with words of profanity. They were big personalities in the area and known to frequent the local taverns, in which some "roughhousing" occasionally took place. Cap—who could be a little crude—got beat up badly after one of those occasions. Somebody ambushed him on his way home from Gann Valley, and he received injuries that needed medical care.

Gus and Cap's house on the ranch was beautiful. Even though I was not there often, I remember it was furnished in the most modern furniture. The bottom story of the house was built into a hill and housed a double garage with a door to the kitchen, which opened into a spacious dining area and living room. They had running water and a bathroom on that floor. The second floor had bedrooms and another bathroom. There was a third story used for parties and dances. It was just one big room with a bar. Grandma Gunderson was their housekeeper. Some years they held the Gunderson family Christmas party there—with Santa Claus. My brother and I looked forward to a trip to the ranch with great anticipation. We loved going to the Gunderson ranch!

I have a vague recollection, as a child, of sitting on Gus Gunderson's lap. He gave us kids candy and gum, and teased all of us. Gus was killed in an automobile accident when I was still very young. I have no recollection of the circumstances, and I never knew him very well.

After Gus' accident, Cap married Jessie, a beautiful redhead from the Gann Valley area. She was a musician. She had a son, Bob, whom Cap adopted. In about 1938 Cap and Jessie had a son together by the name of Roger. He was a cute little redhead with a colorful vocabulary, which he used to entertain the ranch hands. I remember a few black and blue spots on my legs that I received from Roger's cowboy boots. He was a force to be reckoned with but we loved him anyway. Regretfully, I lost contact with him as we grew older.

Jim's brother Sam owned a beautiful blue panel truck that he stocked with products to sell to the local farm and ranch wives around Jerauld County. He had a special gift for conversation, befitting a salesman, especially aimed at making sales to these ladies. He complimented them on their looks, on their house, and their beautiful children. Kate said he had the "gift of gab."

He had customized his panel truck with special shelves on which he stacked everything he could possibly fit inside. There were no passenger seats except in front, and when he opened the back doors we children stood wide-eyed, awed by the variety of products. We also knew he had treats for us somewhere in there.

We curious children followed him into the truck and questioned him profusely about what each product was, and what possible use it had. We followed each and every step he took and examined every object he held, asking a million questions. Sam never missed a beat. Stories—made up, and true—tumbled from his mouth as he worked, mesmerizing us while he filled his basket of goodies to take inside. His intention was to show them and sell them, and not to return them to the panel truck. He was Mr. Personality, PLUS! He said, "Hi, Kate! How are you today? Gosh, Kate, you look great today. I have some new skin cream with me that I think you would really like. I only have a few I saved for my special customers, like you. I'm gonna give you a special price, just because you are my sister-in-law; but don't tell anybody else. This is just between you and me."

Kate replied, "Well, how much is it? Let me try it first." Sam replied, "Absolutely. I happen to have a sample. And I want to show you my lemon extract, too. I know you are the best cook in this neighborhood, so I saved these special flavorings to offer to you on discount today. Jim always raves about your delicious lemon pies. Nobody in this neighborhood can bake lemon pies like you do."

He went on until my mother had a whole variety of little kitchen tools and extracts that would no doubt "please Jim." I sat on the edge of my chair with the introduction of each new product, licking my sucker, and admiring my uncle Sam. My mother knew exactly what was going on but she wanted Sam to be successful; after all, he was her brother-in-law. She often took a lemon pie to Sam and Grandma when she visited them in town. If Grandma ever needed help she knew "Katie would come running."

On some visits to Grandma, she would exclaim in her Norwegian accent, "Uffda, Kate, you need to put some stockings on that child! She's gonna freeze! Oi yoi ya meg!!" I guess that meant something like, "Oh, my gosh!" Kate dearly loved Grandma Gunderson and told stories about her, both funny and touching, and spoke about what a beautiful, caring Christian woman she was.

After Cap and Jessie married, Selmar invited his mother to come live in his home in Wessington Springs. Selmar was a good-hearted guy. Grandma Gunderson suffered from rheumatism and needed a lot of help. Selmar took good care of her until her death, probably for about eight years. I think I was eight or nine years old when Grandma Gunderson died.

TWENTY-SIX

Norwegian Lutherans

KATE'S IN-LAWS, Claus and Sena Gunderson, were founding members of the Salem Lutheran Church, a little country church in the Norwegian community located southwest of Wessington Springs, SD, near Crow Lake. Jim's sister Ida, and her husband Ed Renanado, and daughter Bernice were also members, as were Carl and Ruth Gunderson, Jim's brother and wife. A worship service was held every two or three weeks in the Norwegian language. A few years later the congregation became part of a four-point, all-rural parish along with other small Norwegian congregations north and east of Wessington Springs.

When the congregation was still young, Jim and Kate began to attend worship services with their relatives at Salem. Kate didn't understand a word of the service because it was done in Norwegian, but the relatives urged them to continue attending, so they did. The women invited her to attend ladies aid, but they spoke Norwegian at that function also. Even though she couldn't understand anything that was said, the ladies treated her so nicely that she just continued to go to their meetings. Besides, they were wonderful cooks and she said, "I surely did enjoy the lunch!"

One night at the church council meeting, Carl Gunderson brought up the possibility of hiring Kate to become the church pianist. His wife, Ruth, currently served in that capacity. He informed the council that Kate was a real good piano player and he thought she would do a great job. Kate didn't understand why he did that. She thought maybe he didn't want Ruth to be playing the piano at home. Perhaps Ruth herself wanted to quit. Nobody ever really knew for sure, but the council agreed to hire Kate to be the pianist if she agreed.

The songs in the Lutheran Hymnal were difficult to play! Kate was not at all sure she could learn to play them, but in her words, "I took the bait." She had only taken one year of piano lessons while attending high school in Springfield, but she practiced often and learned a lot about hymn playing in a short period of time. She said the congregation was very encouraging and not at all critical. Kate's job became a whole lot easier when the congregation decided to hold the services in English.

TWENTY-SEVEN

We Need a Choir

KATE FOUND it exciting to be involved in the church, and the more she did the more she wanted to do. As she became more comfortable in her church life she noticed that musical abilities seemed very strong among the voices she heard.

Her thoughts turned to starting a church choir. Not having any prior experience with this, she had some doubts. She wasn't sure she was really capable of developing a church choir but it just felt like the right thing to do, so she held a meeting and those attending were enthusiastic about the prospect of a church choir. They decided to meet Friday evenings for practice, and to rotate so they would practice at a different home each week. At first, they sang simple hymns out of the church hymnal, mostly just the melody. If anyone could sing another harmonizing part, such as alto, tenor, or bass, Kate encouraged them to do so. They were sounding good and the congregation was appreciative of their efforts. They invested in some books that looked as though the vocal parts were somewhat easier than the Lutheran Hymnal. Practice began on all four parts and soon they sounded like a real choir!

The very first song they tackled in all four parts was "Trust and

Obey." She thought their finest achievement was on a piece called "On Fallen Snow," composed and arranged by F. Melius Christiansen. This number became an annual tradition at Christmas. It featured bass voices—Kenny Fagerhaug and Leo Bergeleen had voices that stood out among the many talented male voices. My brother Merrill also became an excellent bass singer.

Kate was constantly amazed at the musical gifts possessed by the choir members. They sang the parts easily without much practice. The most challenging part was tenor. Those singers had to work hard but they persisted and were successful in learning their part.

The choir was something all the youth hoped to participate in as they grew up in the church, waiting eagerly for Kate to invite them be part of the choir. The youngest members would sit next to seasoned singers in order to learn how to sing a part, such as alto, or tenor, or bass. No one was denied the opportunity to sing based on an audition—this choir accepted everyone who wanted sing. Some were more talented than others but no one was ever criticized for singing off key. If they were doing their best that was good enough for all.

The choir performed several cantatas that were quite challenging. Once mastered, we sang them for our church first, and then went to other churches in the parish to perform for them. We had guests come to our performances at Salem Lutheran from other community churches in the area. Our choir had a reputation for producing great music. The names of choir members as Kate remembered them were Bergeleens, Fagerhaugs, Lillehaugs, Johnsons (two families), Hainys, Specks, Crists, Manske, Dammons, Wilsons, (two families) Reeses, Stolens, Boyds, Moldrems, Petersons (two families), Schulenbergers, Renando, and Gundersons.

My dad Jim always took our family to choir practice. This became a weekly social event for the participating families. No one got babysitters for their kids in those days; they always took the kids along, or one parent would stay home with them. Most often, the husbands or fathers who didn't sing—including my dad—played cards, usually Whist, during the rehearsals. The wives who didn't sing would help prepare the lunch that always followed practice. The kids who were too young to sing just played games together. I was only three or four years old when my mother started the choir so I grew up with this tradition. It never occurred to me that other families didn't do this.

Salem Church Choir around 1952

It was a common practice in colder weather to go to one of the bedrooms in a home when we arrived to deposit our coats, scarves, gloves, etc. on the bed. As the children tired out during choir practice they would be told to lie down among the coats on the bed. There were many coats so when it was time to go home parents would look between and under all the coats to find their children. Then they would attempt to put the coats, caps and mittens on sleeping children whose little bodies were limp as rags. When they got them in their wraps they slung the child over their shoulder and took them to their car. In the winter, the host farmyard would be full of cars with engines running to warm up, steam rising from the exhausts of each car.

I especially looked forward to choir practice at the Hugo

Peterson home. It was beautiful, with oak woodwork and an open stairway with a landing. Clara Peterson was an immaculate housekeeper and a wonderful cook. She always had special treats for any kids too young to sing with the choir.

Joy, their youngest daughter, was slightly younger than me, but we were great friends. We played with Joy's dolls and also played "dress-up" by dressing in adult women's clothes that Clara had accumulated for Joy. We came down the stairs in our grown up clothes, dolls and purses in hand, hats falling into our eyes, struggling to navigate each step in our oversized, high-heeled shoes. If we made it as far as the first landing without falling, we proceeded down the next flight, until we arrived downstairs to shouts of encouragement and applause from the choir members. That staircase was our runway and we used it often. Later our parents would find us sound asleep in Joy's upstairs bedroom, still half dressed in those "high society clothes," on Joy's bed or in the next room among all the coats.

As we got older, Joy and I both sang in the choir, along with several other youngsters. In the Salem church, youth usually started choir at about twelve years old. There were many in my age group. At one time, I remember counting twenty-six people who performed a cantata.

Calvin Johnson, who was my age, was one of the guys who grew up in the choir. His most humorous memory was when Kate shouted, "Calling all tenors!" They definitely got worked the hardest. He didn't read notes so he memorized his part by ear.

Cal wrote a beautiful piece reflecting on his memories of the choir and the people of Salem Lutheran church:

"... Anything good that I have done, or that I have become, or that I have achieved is because of the nurturing, and the loving, and the caring that was afforded me by the people of Salem ... the people who were never too busy to give of themselves to help the kids understand what was right and good. As a

boy, I learned much from folks in the Salem community just "doing what comes naturally."

There were never any written contracts between parties when something was bought or sold. A handshake was enough bond to assure the parties that the terms would be carried out. It was something that was just understood.

When someone was sick or injured and couldn't work, the entire community would be there, without being asked, to plant or harvest crops, do farm chores, or whatever was needed to be done to help a family over a crisis.

And you, Kate Gunderson, served the community without ceasing, helping us to develop artistically and socially, too, through our weekly choir drills held in the homes of all the choir members. I remember the relentless, "calling all tenors" (and basses, altos, and sopranos, too), until we got it right. And then it was time for fellowship over a cup of coffee and a sandwich. Chairs were stacked, rugs rolled up, and the remainder of the evening was devoted to the Virginia Reel. Then there were the Bergeleens, and the Fagerhaugs, who never refused to pick up the guitars and the mandolins to entertain us. I was totally enthralled by Leo Bergeleen's "Civet Cat Song" and George Bergeleen telling us about "Truthful Bill" with Inez, Gladys, Kenneth, and Karl picking, strumming, and singing to their accompaniment.

When I left the country and became a "city slicker" I thought my life changed drastically, but as I reflect back on some of the experiences I have had in my life since Salem, I know that all the good things that have happened to me go back to all the good folks in that little community southwest of Wessington Springs (SD).

Salem has never let me down. Thank you for allowing me to be a part of you. You will always be a part of me."

Cal currently resides with his wife in Orange County, California. He still sings in the choir at his church.

TWENTY-EIGHT

Traditions

IN THE EARLY days of Salem Lutheran Church, men sat on one side of the church and women sat on the other for worship services. This was a Norwegian tradition and was strictly followed by members of the church.

When Jim agreed to care for the children during the service so that Kate could be the pianist, he only had men around him for help with the children if he needed it. He laughed as he described the situation. "Merrill sat quietly through the service—he was a little gentleman—but Gayle was a different story; she could not stop wiggling." He said I liked to talk to the men behind him, and when he finally gained control of that situation I tried to get the attention of those in the row ahead. I mussed Jim's hair and made his tie crooked. I became known as the little "wiggle worm." With help from his pew partners, though, he met the challenge.

Kate said, "It was good for him to see what I had to put up with all the time."

Apparently, I never quite got over being a wiggle worm during worship. As the church pianist, Kate sat in the front pew near the piano. As I got older I sat with her. When I reached the age of five or six, Kate thought she could trust me to sit with my friend in a pew further behind. During the sermon my friend and I became bored and started whispering and snickering. Kate turned around, and with her finger to her lips warned me to quiet down, several times! It didn't happen; I didn't respond favorably. Suddenly she stood and walked back to our pew, retrieved me by my arm, and marched me to the front pew to sit beside her, where she could keep me quiet and respectful. The preacher continued to preach, trying not to notice, and managed to keep his train of thought throughout the whole disturbance. All were impressed Kate had taken a visible stand for respect.

My behavior in church was called into question again when I was about ten years old. It happened on a beautiful summer after-noon when the Ladies Aid was meeting in the basement of the church. I had been playing the piano for several years and my latest accomplishment for fun on the piano was to learn a then-popular hit, a song called "*Sioux City* Sue." I played it so often that I had memorized it.

My girlfriends and I were amusing ourselves in the sanctuary while the ladies met downstairs. I thought it would nice if we had some music and proceeded to play "Sioux City Sue" on the piano. The other girls knew the song and we were all having a wonderful time singing loudly and merrily. Once again, my mother suddenly appeared, and once again I was relocated to a church pew. She then informed me I had interrupted the pastor's prayer and there was no further need for "that kind of music" in the sanctuary, especially "*Sioux City Sue*"! Kate had again demonstrated the meaning of respect, and it was becoming quite clear to me, and to my companions.

I recall Kate had a conversation with my dad Jim about the seating arrangement in church. She had a problem with the men on one side and the women on the other, but I don't recall that she discussed it with anyone except him. I have often wondered if she visited with some of the younger women about it. I have a feeling she was quietly planting the seed of change.

Kenneth Fagerhaug and Gladys Bergeleen—a young couple who were active members of our church—got married. The first Sunday morning following their marriage, they came into the church and sat together, as a couple, on the ladies' side of the church. I well remember the gasps and the looks from the congregation at the audacity of this young couple who dared to defy tradition by sitting together. What was this world coming to?

From that time on, each young couple, as they married, sat together. It was not long before all the families began to sit together. We were all happier with that arrangement, and that was how it stayed.

I find it both strange and humorous how old traditions die and new ones begin.

TWENTY-NINE

Christmas Traditions

CHRISTMAS CAROLING WAS a favorite tradition at Salem Lutheran Church, and anyone in a neighboring community was welcome to join us. It was another opportunity for social gathering that might include participants from the whole area. Even though we didn't publicize the event, the neighborhoods always seemed to know which night we were coming. We carolers often numbered twenty or more.

Kate and Jim spread the word to meet at a given place, and then we visited people living in that area to sing Christmas carols. When someone in the neighborhood spotted the motorcade of cars traveling by their house, they passed word by telephone that "the carolers are in the neighborhood. We saw the cars go by. You'll see them soon."

We quietly parked in a spot near the farmhouse we intended to serenade, and circled around the outside of the house. The idea was to surprise the family with a mini-concert of Christmas music. When Kate or Gladys Fagerhaug gave the signal, we opened with a high-energy carol, such as "Joy to the World." So many voices created enough sound that the residents would appear at the door and greet us with goodies for all.

Most families invited us inside for treats and for warmth. We stood around, the house crowded full, and sometimes sang more carols as we enjoyed special treats offered by our hosts. It seemed they had heard a rumor that the Salem Choir would be out and about that night and had prepared for us. Wishing them a Merry Christmas, we proceeded to other homes in the area. The evening ended at one of the caroler's houses for coffee or hot chocolate, games and fellowship.

Several times each year we held a choir party. We practiced singing for about an hour and then the Bergeleens and Fagerhaugs got their guitars and mandolins tuned to the piano and we chose partners to dance the Virginia Reel. We chose a home that had a large room where furniture could be pushed against the walls and still have room for the musicians. These parties proceeded into the early morning hours, only stopping long enough to eat lunch. We played other games periodically but always ended with the Virginia Reel. We still talk about the fun we had at those parties and share memories.

THIRTY

Lutefisk

ANYONE WHO CLAIMS Norwegian ancestry knows about lutefisk. It is a Nordic dish that originated in Sweden, Denmark and Norway, though some people have questioned the authenticity of that statement.

There is one story that claims the Irish put lye in the Vikings fish barrels hoping to poison them. Instead the Vikings found they really liked the fish treated that way so it became tradition to soak the raw fish in lye before cooking. Another story says that about half the Norwegians migrated to America to escape the hated lutefisk, and the other half came to spread the gospel of lutefisk. Actually, lutefisk is dried cod that has been soaked in a lye solution for several days to rehydrate it. It is then rinsed with cold water to remove the lye solution, and boiled or baked. It is usually served with copious amounts of butter.

Nordic families throughout the Midwest—where many of the Norwegian immigrants settled—have a custom of eating lutefisk at Christmas, along with other Nordic foods such as lefse.

When I was a child, the Salem Lutheran ladies held a lutefisk supper every fall at our church. They planned ahead for several months, volunteering for certain duties or to furnish foods that paired well with the lutefisk. The women were spectacular cooks and baked beautiful desserts. Some were really expert at making Norwegian pastries such as flatbread, fattigman, krumkake, and many other Scandinavian foods. Of course, lutefisk was offered as the main item, but the ladies provided alternative choices such as meatballs served with mashed potatoes and gravy, vegetables and/or salad, along with many Scandinavian pastries and desserts.

A huge amount of butter was served with the lutefisk. The ladies churned their own butter, using cream from their milk cows. They served delicious pickles, both sweet and dill, which they canned from cucumbers grown in their garden. Some ladies brought beet pickles, using beets grown in their gardens. Several ladies were gifted in baking breads, and didn't disappoint the guests. The pies were beautiful and the most delicious found anywhere in the countryside. At least we all thought so.

These lutefisk suppers were famous for miles around and were always well attended. Many people came from the Wessington Springs community, Gann Valley, and the Crow Lake area to enjoy the delicious meal. Sometimes the entire sanctuary was filled with people waiting to be seated downstairs, and with other folks who had finished their meal and were socializing.

An event of this magnitude required the husbands as helpers. Everyone planned for the success of the lutefisk supper. In the earliest years, there was no electricity in the church so certain families furnished lighting with their gas lanterns for later in the evening. There was no running water and no indoor bathroom. A considerable amount of water was hauled in by the men, usually in 10-gallon cream cans. The ladies were somewhat crowded when pulling off an event like this—even just for our own congregation. The church kitchen measured about 9' by 12' and had an outside entrance with several steps down to its location in the basement. There was a window for a serving counter on the side facing the large part of the basement.

The cooking range was located on the far side of the kitchen, upon which huge enamel coffee pots were perking from the heat of the range. It was almost as if the big coffee pots were an extension of the range because we never saw them anywhere else. Norwegian cooks were famous for their egg coffee and wouldn't dream of serving coffee without adding freshly cracked eggs stirred into the coffee grounds. Everyone raved about how special their coffee was.

There was a gigantic round ugly furnace located in one corner of the basement. The ladies were extremely clever about camouflaging it. They managed to turn an ugly basement into a beautiful setting for their meal with a splash of fall colors. The tables were beautifully set, with fall flowers and a pure white tablecloth adorning each table.

Everyone had a job to do and it was coordinated in a timely manner. I don't remember any disagreement among the workers, nor any cross words or criticism. I remain amazed at their accomplishment and the fun they had together

Kate loved this activity and she and Jim were heavily committed to its success. Each year we all looked forward to the coming year's event. The families were close, and we who were children then thought for years that we were all cousins—and of course, many of us were. This event drew us even closer.

A few years later the ladies aid decided to serve the lutefisk dinner at the Lutheran church in Wessington Springs. That church had running water, indoor bathrooms, and the location was more favorable. Meal preparation was easier and more convenient because the kitchen was much larger and more modern.

Kate had recently purchased a large pressure cooker to can vegetables and fruits, and even some kinds of meats. The cooking process was shortened considerably by using this cooker. She offered it to the ladies to cook potatoes for the dinner. They were pleased to use anything that would work more quickly and be more convenient.

I was in the basement with the other children of the cooking ladies when we heard a small explosion. Some of the ladies had attempted to remove the lid of the cooker a little too soon. There was a high degree of activity around my mother—they seemed to be wrapping her in towels. They rushed her out of the basement to the doctor. She had been severely burned by the steam escaping from the cooker. After being treated, she returned to the dinner for a short time but we left early. Kate suffered a lot of pain at first but she healed miraculously well, and rather quickly. She always felt fortunate that she was only burned badly on one of her arms. That arm remained very sensitive to cold temperatures for a long time but there were no worse residual complications.

The lutefisk dinners continued in town for a few more years, but then the ladies decided to make money in other ways. To this day, though, when someone mentions the lutefisk suppers we all remember something wonderful about them, and share many fond memories of that time in our lives.

THIRTY-ONE

Luther League

THERE WERE three churches in our Lutheran parish, located about twenty miles apart. We shared a pastor who lived in Wessington Springs, the central location. It was not possible for him to preach in all three churches every Sunday morning, so each church in the parish had a family Luther League. A meeting was held every other Sunday evening at Salem Lutheran Church on the Sundays that we had no worship service. All ages participated.

Kate and Gladys Fagerhaug were our coaches and advisors. When piano accompaniment was needed for singers, Kate was always there. Gladys coached the singers, especially at Christmas time. Someone was appointed to read a short lesson found in a Lutheran publication. Gladys and Kate were available for suggestions about literally everything that took place.

Our family Luther League prepared us through personal experience how to be involved in and lead a meeting similar to worship. Kate and Gladys were role models and teachers who taught us how to cooperate, be responsible, think creatively—and very often how to solve problems quickly and think on our feet. We learned to listen, negotiate, and appreciate another opinion—all skills needed by effective leaders. Our faith concepts were also enhanced as we learned to respect and love our congregational family.

Kate and Gladys, Luther League coaches and advisors

THIRTY-TWO

Salem Lutheran 50 Years

KATE WAS among those honored at the fiftieth anniversary celebration for Salem—as the choir leader and pianist. History bears out the fact that she organized the choir in 1937, with eight people attending. In 1957, the 50th year, it was noted that at least one hundred people had participated at one time or another during those years.

Gladys Fagerhaug was also a major influence in the church as a youth leader. She directed the annual Youth Christmas Program, which included lots of music. Kate was the pianist. These two ladies continued to creatively direct and promote special musical events and programs at Salem Lutheran until the late 1950s, when the church was integrated with the other churches of the parish into one central church in Wessington Springs, named Our Savior's Lutheran Church. They didn't stop volunteering at that time; they continued helping wherever they were needed.

Gladys was the mother of Kyle Evans, a well-known South Dakota country music artist who, in 1969 created the music group Kyle Evans & the Company Cowboys. They were favorite entertainers for rodeos and dances in the region. Kyle also performed solo and with other country music stars at professional performances and pageants. Kyle's brother, Lennis Fagerhaug, double cousin Brian Bergeleen (son of Karl and Inez Bergeleen)—all members of Salem Lutheran Church—and Dale Schimke were original members of the group. Brian still entertains solo in the local area, and occasionally with Lennis and/or other family members. Kyle died from injuries he received in a motorcycle accident in 2001.There is a memorial to Kyle located three miles east of Wessington Springs on US Highway 34, which was the location of the accident, and another located one mile west of the town. They are maintained by family members and friends.

NATIONAL LUTHERAN COUNCIL WORKERS

Salem Lutheran Congregation was privileged to have two of their young ladies in the work of the National Lutheran Council.

Mrs. Clifford Bergeleen, nee Doris Shulenberger, and Mrs. Kenneth Fagerhaug, nee Gladys Bergeleen, joined the National Lutheran Council in 1943. They served as Defense Area Visitors who worked throughout the United States organizing a church away from home for those who left their homes to work in defense plants.

CHOIR HISTORY

"Oh come, let us sing unto Jehovah;
Let us make a joyful noise to the rock of our salvation."

Mrs. James Gunderson

This is the challenge that has been met by the choir of Salem congregation through the years.

In 1937 Mrs. James Gunderson invited eight young people to her home for choir practice. From this beginning the choir has continued for 20 years.

Through the years about 100 persons have sung in the choir, and practice has been held almost every week barring bad weather. The choir practices have served as a time for Christian fellowship and have done much to keep our young men and women active in their Christian faith.

Times change, babies are born, people die, technical inventions happen, farms are deserted, new homes are built. Generations later, I am able to observe the influence those early settlers had on the families who remain in that community. As a child, that community was my universe, and I am grateful. It is always a joy to reconnect with them.

My mother Kate not only served as a community leader, but was responsible for helping move many activities forward at Salem Lutheran Church. While teaching full-time at the school, she also held the roles of housewife, mother, part-time student, and was both a leader and a participant in multiple church activities. She served as an example of leadership, commitment, and dedication. Like the famous bunny on TV ads, she just didn't quit!

THIRTY-THREE

Kate the Teacher

KATE TAUGHT school for nearly thirty years. All her experience was in rural one-room schools attended by students in grades 1-8, except her last two years when she taught in Gann Valley, SD.

One of the years Kate taught at Happy Hill School there were twenty students. I was in college at that time, but I remember visiting her school during my Christmas vacation and I gained a new respect for her ability as a teacher. To teach effectively Kate had to be emotionally strong, well organized, creative, flexible, and observant. She had to be firm but sympathetic and well prepared to meet each new situation. Several students graduated from eighth grade that year, and the enrollment declined in later years, but Happy Hill had children in every grade for a long time.

Gann Valley was a very small town and school enrollment there was also small—similar to when Kate attended as a student. Kate taught ten students in grades seven and eight. She enjoyed the luxury of a custodian to keep her room clean, and she appreciated hot lunches prepared by the school cook. She enjoyed her experience at Gann Valley and spoke fondly of it being a wonderful way to end her teaching career.

Rural school conditions slowly improved after the "dirty thirties." Potbellied stoves were replaced by furnaces. At first the furnaces burned only coal, but later they were fueled by propane, which burned much cleaner. School districts furnished better desks for students, and more and better books. School buildings were repaired and improved. Some townships consolidated their schools so there were more students attending two-room schools that had more conveniences. Electricity and running water became available, and sometimes the two-room schools had someone prepare noon lunches for them.

Kate pictured with some of her students at Powell school. Back row L-R: Donna Thompson Steineke, Norma Hurley, Kate, Myrna Swanson, Arlene Rudeen. Front row L-R: Mel Radke, Don Hurley, Verla Radke, Melvin Hurley.

Kate had a very creative side and she was especially appreciative of music. She liked drama and had a special talent for reciting poetry. All of these things were integrated into her method of teaching. Kate believed she needed to teach the whole child, and discovered some special talents in her students, which she encouraged and nurtured. I was her student for a few years. I know her teaching methods varied according to the learning styles that she discovered among her students.

Kate's daughter Gayle with her husband Jack Cranston

Inspired by my mother Kate, I (Gayle) became an elementary teacher in the 1950s, teaching in city schools around the state. I learned from her the importance of finding the learning curve for each student, and the importance of listening and encouraging each student without being critical. At the same time, discipline and respect were also important, and this became much more apparent when I had my own classroom. I attended continuing education classes and workshops in the late 1970s that empha-sized "individualizing" in classrooms. I remember thinking that my mother, as well as other rural school teachers, had discovered "individualizing" many years earlier.

I married Jack Cranston, a graduate of Huron College, in 1956. He became a school superintendent in small schools in South Dakota. Jack died in 2001 but former students still remember and speak fondly of him. Those small communities were wonderful places to live, and in which to raise our children.

Kate encouraged singing and speaking in school because she felt it was a confidence-builder. She always coached her students in performance. She gave special attention to how the children expressed themselves. "You need to put some expression into it!" she said. She remembered how her dad had coached her about how to stand and to always smile when performing. Kate urged us to sing our music with great enthusiasm.

School programs were very important to students and their parents in rural schools. Students got new clothes to wear for these programs. The guys all got haircuts and wore ties. The girls had special hairdos and ribbons in their hair. Everyone wanted to look their Sunday best for the big event. The parents were supportive of whatever Mrs. Gunderson said. They seemed to understand she was doing her best to give their children a well-rounded education.

School programs were also an opportunity to make money to finance a special school trip. The mothers would make cakes and pies to be auctioned off or sold by the piece. Box socials were common. A box social was an event where the girls and women in the community fixed a special lunch which they packed in a box. The box was beautifully decorated and sold at auction to the highest bidder, which included eating lunch with the creator of the box. Sometimes a box would be sold for a ridiculous price so the buyer could eat with a special young lady. The married men usually bought their wife's box, if they recognized it. It was fascinating and entertaining for the school children to watch the auctioneer and the bidders.

Following the auction everyone ate with the person whose box they bought and the rest of the evening was social. Sometimes there was card playing, but mostly everyone just sat around and visited. It was a great time for the neighborhood to get together and enjoy each other's company. The proceeds from the auction and the sales of cake and pie were used later for a special day trip for the students, or sometimes to buy a special piece of equipment for them.

Some of Kate's students went on to become teachers of math and science and music. Some went on to prestigious careers in engineering. Many continued to farm. Many former students remained in contact with Kate when they were adults, offering words of appreciation for the experiences she provided when she was their teacher. They almost always mentioned the school programs in their conversations with her later.

On the following pages find a copy of a letter from Kate's former student Donna Thompson Steineke.

A Tribute to a Teacher
Kathryn (Kate) Gunderson
February 5, 2008

Mrs. Gunderson, Your smile lit up our days.   You loved us and you loved your job. There were many things you did for us all. To this one-room school house you arrived early to stoke up the fire in the furnace and haul in the water for us to drink and use in the wash basin. The chart revealed what chores were ours for the week. Black boards needed to be cleaned, chalk board erasers were cleaned by pounding them on the cement where they left their white rectangular boxes of dust, and floors were swept and the school kept tidy. Oh, do you remember when the parents got you a kerosene stove because you thought we needed a warm meal at noon. My favorite was your cooked potatoes covered with pork n'beans. Besides having us come up to sit on our little red chairs for reading and reciting our sums, you taught us to sing. Those were wonderful Christmas programs that you orchestrated and to display our talents.   At recess you came out to play Pump, Pump, Pole Away and Anti-I-Over. All of these were great blessings for us all and my mother declared that you were the best teacher in Jerauld county.

However, these blessings were only the backdrop to the biggie for me . In 1944, four little first grade girls were entrusted to your care. One of them, me, you told my mother, came to school to have fun. Your work was cut out for you and you settled right into the task. How do you get a little fun-loving imp to settle down and do her studies well. Remember, I embarrassed you when I, with my mischievous brown eyes dancing, told one of my fellow students, "Eat your bread crusts so you'll get hair on your chest."   It was out before you had a chance to stop it. But you know it wasn't me who got into trouble at home; it was my Dad for telling me that when I didn't eat my bread crusts.   But it didn't matter I didn't get scolded at home, because I wanted to please you more than anything. The key to that desire was, I heard you tell my mother, to praise what I did well. It wasn't until just this year that I gained an understanding of why that worked so well with me. While studying Gary Chapman's book, _The Five Love Languages_, I realized that my main love love language was "words of affirmation." I know that back then praise was not given to children for fear they would become prideful. But you took the risk. I felt loved and wanted to please you and I could see that I could please you by learning and so I morphed into a student who loved to learn. Thank you for the opportunity to call you teacher for four wonderful years. Besides my parents, you, my grandma and my aunt had a positive and profound influence on who I became as a person. These pleasant memories of our school days together have been an enjoyable companion for many years.

I want you to know that I became a teacher. Seventh and eighth graders were my charges for 22 years. You impacted my teaching deeply because ingrained in my conscience was the thought to look for the positive in these students. I sensed your loving presence as I passed this gift on. I sometimes wished that some of the students I had would have had a Mrs. Gunderson their first four years. Their school lives would have been much richer.

Before I close, I do need to tell you that I'm sorry for the couple times I really disappointed you. The one was an accident and I'm sorry I wasn't more careful. The other was planned, but the implications of my actions wasn't thought out. I heard my mother say that you realized when you spanked me that it wasn't an effective punishment. Bingo, you were right again. (It was really administered so softly that I was puzzled and didn't know what it was until I saw your face.) But what you didn't realize is that I was punished when I perceived the disappointment and anger written on your face framed by red hair. Facial expressions are a dialect of "words of affirmation." A loving smile speaks love and being deprived of that was the greatest punishment you could have delivered. I'm sorry I disappointed you.

However what I have really wanted to tell you all these years is the positive influence you've had on my life. At my mother's funeral in 97 I sought you out to tell you that. But somehow the conversation got side tracked and I was never satisfied that I got the message to you. Now, I'm ending up sending this letter to your new address in heaven. Again, thank you and good bye until we meet again.

Your grateful student, Donna

Gayle, this is my gift to your mother, and I'm forwarding it to you, her heir.

May our heavenly father comfort you and bring you peace at this time.

Donna Thompson Steineke

Our sympathy, Dale and Donna Steineke

THIRTY-FOUR

Young Citizens League

THE YOUNG CITIZENS League (YCL) was an organization in which most rural South Dakota schools participated while Kate was teaching. It was started in the 1930s as part of a national program focused on building character and patriotism through education and student experiences. Students were encouraged to do something each day that highlighted shared responsibility in a group or community, and caring about others. Patriotism, and "helping Uncle Sam" were also emphasized, especially during WWII. It was a daily exercise on how to be a good citizen. Kate encouraged active participation in YCL by all students.The students elected officers every month and duties were assigned to be done around the school every day. Students created projects, under the direction of the teacher, that related to what America was experiencing as a country and what the country represented as a democracy. All students were expected to memorize the YCL creed, and the official song was sung at every meeting.

I remember a YCL project to assist and support the WWII efforts. We went to a place where milkweeds were growing and spent an afternoon gathering milkweed pods. The bags of pods, which were picked by school children all over Jerauld County, were taken to a central area from which they were shipped to the US military who used them in making flotation devices for servicemen. We also made scrapbooks promoting patriotism and honoring soldiers serving in the war. Some of these scrapbooks were later displayed at the county fair, along with YCL projects from many other schools in Jerauld County.

Students attend Jerauld County Young Citizens League in Wessington Springs SD

Every school sent YCL delegates to a county-wide meeting in the spring. Students from all the county schools were invited to participate in a songfest at this time also. We practiced the songs at our own school prior to the county chorus getting together, and we had a director who helped our large group perform for the public. It was quite a thrill to be part of such a big sound and a memorable event. The children from the city schools in Wessington Springs were also invited to participate if they desired.

I had the honor of presiding over the Jerauld County YCL meeting as an eighth grader. I had been elected to that position the previous year. I was extremely nervous and it challenged my ability to lead but it was a good learning experience—and Kate was there to coach me.

YCL PROGRAM

Twentieth Annual Convention.

Call to Order.........President Grohs.........Longfellow School

Song.................America.................Audience
(Remain Standing For The Invocation)
Invocation...........Rev.F.R.Kuegele.........Wess.Springs,S.D.

Salute to the Flag...Led by Norma Jean Hodgson.Schubert School

Y.C.L.Pledge.........Led by Peggy Schaefer....Schaefer School

Address of Welcome...Mr.Hugh Short, Mayor of Wessington Springs.

Response.............Earl Reese.............Fagerhaug School

Rhythm Band.........."Music Around the World"..Plainview School

Reading............."Eight on a Pass".........Maxine Madden.

Selections on the Guitar.....................Lloyd Marken.

Y.C.L.Purpose and Motto..Jean Powell.........Linn School.

Young Citizens& Code of Ethics.............. Christensen Sch.

Piano Selection..."Star of the Sea"......... Peggy Schaefer.

Reading......"Clubby"....Ona Jean Bunde..... Lane Cons. Sch.

Verse Choir--..."The Shoemaker's Elves"....... Powell School.

Selections on the Tonettes.................. Happy Hollow Sch.

Solo......."Sing Me To Sleep"...Keo Schoff...Wess.Springs Ind.

Tricks by the Magician.....Mr.Fromke......... Plankinton, S.D.

Y.C.L.March Song............................ The Audience.

Oh, up from every valley   We march and we sing,our voices
And down from every crest,   Young citizens are we;   (ring;
We come, thy loyal children,   Leagued in a host whose watch-
By all thy favors blest,   words are
To pledge our firm allegiance, Youth, courage, loyalty.
America, to thee,   Hailing our nation's banner
Thy guardians of tomorrow,   Afloat in the sunlit sky;
By mountain, plain and sea.   Which thru hopes and fears,
                                Thru future years,
                                We will hold evermore on high.

April 27, 1946.

YCL Program 1946

THIRTY-FIVE

A New Career

LATE IN KATE'S teaching career she decided to try her hand at a different profession. She had a strong math background, was a good problem solver, and was interested in a job with a new set of responsibilities. After much deliberation she ran for Jerauld County Treasurer. She won the election.

VOTE FOR

☒ K. E. Gunderson

DEMOCRATIC CANDIDATE
for Re-Election to the Office of

JERAULD COUNTY TREASURER

YOUR VOTE AND SUPPORT IN THE NOV. 8
ELECTION WILL BE SINCERELY APPRECIATED

Kate was good at this job and she enjoyed it. She had an aptitude for it and liked meeting and conversing with the people. Among the interesting people she met were George and Eleanor McGovern. Kate's political beliefs meshed well with theirs and she spoke with them on several occasions.

She continued as Jerauld County Treasurer for four two-year

terms. When she was defeated for a fifth term, she expected to retire and looked forward to staying home every day with no daily commitments.

Meanwhile, a teacher at one of the rural schools had resigned for health reasons. That school board called Kate, asking if she would consider teaching there for the remainder of the term. She had to make a quick decision. Knowing the job was only temporary, she accepted their offer.

Kate had attended summer school yearly while still teaching, and took workshops and seminars. She had attended night classes to earn credits toward a college degree and was very close to the total needed. My husband Jack and I strongly urged her to consider completing the few remaining requirements she needed for her degree. She heard about a group of teachers in the area who were carpooling to Huron from Wessington Springs twice each week for night classes at Huron University. Kate was invited to join them and share expenses. She completed one course in that night class and attended summer school to complete the necessary number of credits. Kate graduated from Huron University with a B.A. degree at age sixty-five. When graduation day arrived my family and in-laws, along with other family and friends, proudly watched her walk across the stage to receive her college diploma. What an accomplishment! We were so proud of her.

Kate had friends teaching in Wessington Springs who suggested she apply for an open position. She went to the Office of the Super-intendent to apply. She was received by a very professional super-intendent who gave her the short answer: "No." She was not qualified—because of her age. They could not consider her because she was "too old." He said it was school policy, no exceptions. What a loss for the school district! Not only was she in excellent health but her many years of experience qualified her to easily handle any class put before her, especially in the lower grades where they had the vacancy.

Kate struggled to handle her disappointment. This was the only time in my life I remember observing her feeling defeated. She had a hard time picking herself up from this blow.

There were no laws regarding age discrimination at that time. She had no alternatives. She finally resigned herself to no future teaching plans.

True to her own beliefs that "everything happens for a reason," and "always look ahead," she "stayed in the buggy" and looked for other job opportunities.

"Each of us has the right to assess the roads which lie ahead and those over which we have traveled, and if the future road looms ominous or unpromising, and the roads back uninviting, then we need to gather our resolve and, carrying only the necessary baggage, step off that road I nto another direction. If the new choice is unpalatable, without embarrassment, we must be ready to change that as well." Maya Angelou

THIRTY-SIX

Other Choices

AVON COSMETICS WAS LOOKING for a representative in the Wessington Springs area. They wanted a "people person" and someone well-known in the rural area. This was something new and different and since Kate knew a lot of people she decided to become an Avon representative.

She was getting used to her new job when the Gann Valley Board of Education offered her a job teaching grades seven and eight.

She was surprised. There were questions. How much did they pay? Would she make enough money for it to be profitable after paying for gas? It was a 20-mile commute one way. Would she have the stamina for this job? How many students? Were they well-behaved? Any behavior problems?

Kate and Jim carefully weighed the pros and cons and concluded she should try it. My dad was very supportive of whatever she wanted. Kate was eager to take this job and excited to once again have the opportunity to teach.

After a few weeks on the job she discovered she loved everything about it. Her class was small, around ten students. They were all cooperative and willing learners. Again she enjoyed the services of a janitor and a school cook. The commute was relaxing for the most part. She seldom had to deal with icy roads and snow. When they offered her a contract for another year, she signed it.

At the end of her second year at Gann Valley, the board announced the school was closing and all students would be bussed to Wessington Springs. Kate was somewhat disappointed but understood that financially it made perfect sense for Gann Valley to consolidate with the Wessington Springs Public Schools.

As she reflected on her circumstances, she seemed at peace. Her college education had been used in some purposeful way. She had a good feeling about retiring from teaching, and looked forward to new ideas and different opportunities.

Kate had continued to sell Avon on a limited basis while teaching, and she now pursued that business fulltime. She traveled from Wessington Springs to many rural homes each week to call on farm wives. They welcomed her into their homes, offered her coffee, and visited with her as if she was an old friend. They called on the telephone to order if she had not called on them personally. Kate held open houses at least twice each year and promoted her Avon position by leaving catalogs wherever she went. She was thoroughly enjoying her job in sales and had made some new acquaintances in Jerauld County. It was enjoyable and she earned many sales awards.

After Jim passed away she remarried and lived in the Kimball area. She continued to sell Avon there on a limited basis to some people who were her neighbors in the country. She was ninety years old when she decided to quit her sales career entirely.

THIRTY-SEVEN

Kate the Homemaker

KATE HAD a green thumb and loved growing vegetables to freeze and can. Her garden also included a huge strawberry patch and a patch of hollyhocks that bloomed profusely each year. She also planted smaller flower gardens in various places around the farm.

Kate in her hollyhock garden

Kate loved to cook and bake—she baked bread and delicious cinnamon rolls with sensational caramel topping. Cookies with date or raisin filling were one of her specialties, and Jim and Merrill loved them. She baked pies—both cream pies and double crust. She used the rhubarb from her garden to make many desserts, sometimes combining strawberries or apples with the rhubarb. She used her own farm apples to make apple butter, or sliced and froze them for future baking. She prepared ham, turkey, or roast beef dinners, complete with mashed potatoes and tasty gravy, and corn or beans from her freezer. She spent hours harvesting strawberries and freezing them for topping on ice cream and for jams, jellies, and desserts.

Grandma Kate's Pancakes

Written By: Grandma Kate

---

1 cup flour	2 tablespoons oil
3 level tsp. baking powder	1 egg
1/4 tsp. salt	1 cup milk
2 tablespoons sugar	

In a medium sized mixing bowl combine the first four dry ingredients and mix together.
Add the wet ingredients to the dry ingredients and combine until only a few lumps remain.
Cook on a hot, oiled griddle and enjoy!

Kate's biggest delight was fixing pancakes, and she often spontaneously called the neighbors and invited them over for a pancake supper. She was known as the "Queen of Pancakes." She made an assortment of syrups from her strawberries and chokecherries, as well as offering the option of regular store-bought syrup. Sometimes she made her own version of regular syrup from scratch. Her neighbors raved about her famous pancakes and waffles. Of course, whether it was breakfast or supper, no meal of pancakes or waffles was complete without ham or bacon. Kate and Jim had a supply of frozen meat from animals raised on the Gunderson farm. Kate also had farm-fresh eggs to add into the menu. No one ever went away hungry from her home.

Jim sort of "batched it" during the week when Kate was teaching, but he never complained. He could always find something to eat for lunch. He got so good in the kitchen that he could put together a pretty good meal for some other guy who might be helping out on a given day.

Kate making pancakes with great-grandchildren Quinn Cranston, Cory Cranston (back), Haley Cranston, Brianne Cranston-Miller

On some occasions when we had prepared a meal for unexpected guests at our table, my mother would apologize for the way the house looked. Without change of facial expression, Jim would add, "Some days it looks worse." He was a man of few words, but what he said was often comic relief. In the midst of a meal, while we were passing dishes and filling our plates, he might say, "Just keep one foot on the floor when you are reaching."

Kate loved to have a group of people around her and she loved to cook, so we often had company at our house, planned or unplanned. I recall making trips to the basement for an armload of food from the freezer or canned food from the shelf for her to prepare and put on the table for company.

She most often baked in her old kitchen range and cooked on its top also. She finally updated her stove by adding two burners fueled by propane on one end of the stove. She really appreciated this new-found convenience and used it all the time.

Kate's big pleasure in life was sharing produce she had grown with friends and neighbors, hoping others could use it.

HOME

It takes a heap o' livin' in a house t'make it home,
A heap o' sun an' shadder, an' ye sometimes have t' roam
Afore ye really 'preciate the things ye lef behind,
An' hunger fer 'em somehow, with 'em allus on yer mind.
It don't make any difference how rich ye get t' be,
How much yer chairs an' tables cost, how great yer luxury;
It ain't home t' ye, though it be the palace of a king,
Until somehow yer soul is sort o' wrapped round everything.

Home ain't a place that gold can buy or get up in a minute;
Afore it's home there's got t' be a heap o' livin' in it;
Right there ye've got t' bring 'em up t' women good, an' men;
And gradjerly, as time goes on, ye find ye wouldn't part
With anything they ever used— they've grown into yer heart:
The old high chairs, the playthings, too, the little shoes they wore
Ye hoard; an' if ye could ye'd keep the thumb marks on the door.

Ye've got t' weep t' make it home, ye've got t' sit an' sigh
An watch beside a loved one's bed, an know that Death is nigh;
An' in the stillness o' the night t' see Death's angel come,
An close the eyes o' her that smiled,
An' leave her sweet voice dumb.
Fer these are scenes that grip the heart,
An when yer tears are dried,
Ye find the home is dearer than it was, an' sanctified;
An tuffin' at ye always are the pleasant memories
O' her that was an' is no more—ye can't escape from these.

Ye've got t' sing an' dance fer years, ye've got t' romp an' play,
An learn t' love the things ye have by usin' 'em each day.
Even the roses 'round the porch must blossom year by year
Afore they 'come a part o' ye, suggestin' someone dear

Who used t' love 'em long ago, an' trained 'em jes' t' run
The way they do, so's they would get the early mornin' sun;
Ye've got t' love each brick an' stone from cellar up t' dome:
It takes a heap o' livin' in a house t' make it home.
Edgar Albert Guest

THIRTY-EIGHT
Kate the Organizer

KATE WAS AN ORGANIZER. About every three years—sometimes sooner—she felt it was time for a family reunion. Most of the time she intended the reunions for her siblings and families but sometimes she included invitations to aunts, uncles, and cousins who lived a greater distance away. Most of them lived in Nebraska, Kansas, South and North Dakota, and some had moved to Minnesota, Montana, Colorado and Washington state.

She loved to invite everybody to our farm for the reunion. Sometimes we had fifty or more people. My dad worked for several weeks cleaning the yard and the chicken coops and the other little buildings. He made sure there were places for the kids to play and kept the barn clean so we could get the ponies ready to ride. The horseshoe pit needed to be in good shape, and he mowed and trimmed around the trees by the house. Kate always had a big garden with lots of flowers, so Jim rigged a fence to protect them. He seemed to look forward to the reunions as much as Kate. The neighborhood always knew when there was going to be a grand reunion at the Gunderson farm because it was buzzing with activity and excitement.

All the bedrooms in the farm house were occupied, so we pulled out the hide-a-bed, made beds on the floors for kids, and some could even sleep on the outdoor porch. At no time was Kate happier than when her house was filled with people having fun, kids running in all directions, and her sisters-in-law in the kitchen preparing food with her.

We would wake up to the smell of bacon cooking. Kate was getting ready to make pancakes for the whole "gang," as she called us. She had special chokecherry syrup that she had made herself after gathering the chokecherries from the bushes in the grove of trees behind the house. We grouped and regrouped, laughing and talking at the table as we took our turns eating her delicious breakfast with coffee or tea.

In spite of the fact that we used an outhouse for several of these gatherings (they didn't have running water until after I was married) her family still loved to gather at Kate's for these events. No one complained about the lack of modern conveniences—they all seemed to thoroughly enjoy the entire experience.

There were times when family reunions were held in other places also, but Kate was always consulted about the logistics. One time a reunion was held at Kate's brother Bill's farm, about four miles from the Gunderson farm. One time we traveled to Estelline to a farm where Mary and Elmer Gerth lived. We gathered in Ephrata, WA twice, hosted by my brother Merrill and his wife Dakota; twice in Montana, hosted by my cousin Gary Gerth, and wife Bonnie; and twice we gathered in Seattle hosted by Kate's youngest sister, Lena and husband Arnold Lunnum.

Other memorable reunions were held to honor 50th wedding celebrations in Lake Andes, SD, Farmington, MN, and for Jim and Kate Gunderson at the 4-H Building in Wessington Springs so that community members could attend along with family members.

Several family events were held in the beautiful city park in Wessington Springs. Every family generously furnished food and provided entertainment. We all have great memories of these gatherings and they provided us an opportunity to stay in touch and maintain our relationships over the years. Kate was the "glue" in the family and provided the incentive for the family reunions.

Kate instigated many smaller gatherings of the local Wilson families around Wessington Springs. When Grandma Wilson was alive she joined us; and later we were joined by Jennie and Lois Wilson, widows of Henry and Ira Wilson.

Kate would not let a holiday pass without some kind of get-together, and never passed up an opportunity to celebrate a birthday. She really didn't need a reason. "Sometimes," she said, "it was just because I felt like it."

Jim: Kate's Husband, My Dad

MY DAD JIM was a really quiet guy. He didn't talk much, even at home. He worked hard, was very steady and dependable, and fiercely honest and fair in all things. If he gave his word on something you could depend on him to carry through. He wasn't a "touchy, feely" kind of guy who was giving hugs all the time, but Merrill and I knew he cared about us and he made us feel safe and secure. By the time he had grandchildren he was a bit more verbal and didn't mind showing some open affection to them.

I remember Jim talking to my mother sometimes, but I don't recall that he talked much with us kids until we were young adults, unless we engaged him in conversation. As I look back, I see he had some serious insecurities and relied heavily on Kate for support and encouragement. She was always there as his confidence builder, but there were times when he even doubted her.

When I was growing up our family moved from one farm to another four times in ten years, mainly because my dad didn't believe there was any way he could ever buy a farm. When we made a move it was a major event. We had to move livestock, all the farm machinery, vehicles, and house furnishings. It meant my brother and I would attend a different school with a new teacher and new schoolmates, and there would also be new neighbors. Thankfully, we had good friends and dependable relatives who helped each time we made a move.

Jim, who always had a pipe in his mouth

The last move my family made was in 1948 when I was a ninth grader. This time, Kate persuaded Jim to buy the farm instead of renting again. She told him they had to make a commitment and then focus on accomplishing it. She was not willing to make another move. She reminded him that they were no different than other people who bought farms. She said, "Others do it. We are no different. It isn't easy for anybody, but if others are doing it, we can too."

Jim said "okay" so they made a commitment to purchase the Marten Place, six miles southwest of Wessington Springs.

Jim and Kate went to the Office of the Federal Land Bank to borrow money to purchase the farm. Some of the officials they talked with were highly doubtful they could handle the debt but Kate said, "I'm pretty sure we can. Just give us a chance." The bank did give them a chance. Not only did they pay back all of the original loan, but later they borrowed more money to purchase another eighty acres of land near their pasture to grow and harvest extra hay, and they also paid off that loan.

The final homestead

Our family lived without luxuries like running water and an indoor bathroom, and we were among the very last people in our area to get electricity in our house. My dad always bought used machinery and we always bought used cars. We didn't have nice furniture but interestingly, I don't ever remember feeling deprived or neglected. We were happy and content, and never felt hungry.

Jim and Kate Gunderson, 40th anniversary

FORTY

Gramma Kate and Grampa Jim Stories

WHEN MY BROTHER Merrill and I became young adults—getting married and having babies— Jim and Kate were very generous about helping out with our needs. They helped Merrill and me with unforeseen expenses with our children, and gave generously of their time. They helped care for Merrill and Dakota's children when they lived on the same farm and dearly loved having them nearby. When Merrill and Dakota left that farm, their children Rhonda, Randy, and Dana were still young—their youngest, Sonja, was born in Michigan.

My children spent time on the farm with Kate and Jim in the summer. They remember Kate packing a lunch and hiking with them across the pasture to a grove of trees. Cady Lake was nearby and they hiked around the shores of the lake. They entertained themselves building forts, climbing trees, and just exploring for many hours. Kate helped them find places to explore at first, but after a while they went by themselves and could entertain themselves for an entire afternoon.

They slept on the porch, waking to cooing doves, the sounds of leaves in the breeze, fresh morning air, and the aroma of bacon frying in the house. Gramma Kate greeted them with a cheery "good morning" and sat them down to eat her delicious pancakes with sausage or bacon.

As the grandchildren got older, Grandpa Jim provided a way for them to make money to buy school clothes. He helped them learn how to strip bluegrass. The first year they stripped blue grass he drove the tractor pulling the strippers and they had a chance to see how it was done by helping him load and unload, etc. The next year, Rick, who was about fifteen, drove the tractor pulling the strippers. Carole, about twelve, helped Grampa Jim transfer the seed from the strippers to the pickup. When the pickup box was full it was Carole's job to take the loaded truck to town to have it weighed, and then have it unloaded at another location just outside town.

Carole learned how to drive the pickup truck the day before she was told she would be responsible for taking it to town to unload the seed. The truck had a stick shift on the floor and she had to practice starting and stopping many times. Grampa Jim drove with her to town and showed her where to go to weigh the seed. He pointed out the scale and showed her how to drive onto it. Then they drove to where the seed would be unloaded.

The day she was to take the seed to town, Grampa Jim put her in the driver's seat of the pickup and instructed her to take it to town, all alone! She had to drive four miles on a gravel road, turn onto the main highway for two miles, and turn onto the street leading into town. The scale was located at a lumber yard off the main street into town, and she had to maneuver several turns in order to guide the pickup onto the scale. She waited for the receipt from the clerk and then drove to the outskirts of town where the pickup was unloaded for her. She then returned to the farm to pick up the next load. At first she was terrified she would not remember everything, or that the pickup would stall and she wouldn't be able to start it, or that it might run out of gas. By the third trip she was more comfortable and confident. As the day went on she felt really grown up and important. Rick, too, remembers how much he liked driving the tractor and how he felt grown up. In fact, he began thinking about becoming a farmer someday.

The two of them made several hundred dollars selling the seed and Grampa Jim let them keep it all to buy their school clothes.

Reflecting on the experience gained by the children, the trust placed in them to do these jobs was a big part of growing up—a chance to mature in their thinking and accept responsibility. They never forgot how Grampa Jim trusted them at such an early age.

One time the boys were helping Grampa Jim in the hayfield. He was driving the tractor pulling a mower. Rick was riding on the seat of the rake which was pulled behind the mower. It was his job to dump the hay being raked into windrows. Brad and Barry—Rick's brothers who were much younger—were riding on the rake with Rick. Jim had somehow run over a wasp or bee nest and they began to swarm around the boys. They all jumped off the rake and were trying to run away from the wasps. They were running faster than Grampa Jim on the tractor and passed him. Grandpa Jim, who was contentedly driving and smoking his pipe, suddenly noticed the boys running ahead of him. When he saw the bees chasing the boys he understood what was happening. He also became a part of the escape as the bees were attacking him, too. First, he had to stop the tractor and mower and then he joined the boys running. All four ran until they had outrun the bees, and even though they had a few stings it was better than being attacked by the swarm.

All of the grandchildren have fond memories of Jim and Kate taking them to the dam in the pasture to fish for bullheads. First, they took a pail to the garden to dig up worms for bait. Then they found the fishing poles—the kind made from bamboo with a line attached with a red bobber and a fish hook. They didn't have rods and reels.

They always took a lunch or treats of some kind because it was boring waiting for the fish to bite. Eating was a good way to deal with boredom. When the red bobber bobbed up and down on the water they knew they had a nibble; when it went completely under it was time to jerk the pole up and out of the water. They squealed to see a fish wiggling crazily on the line as it whirled around over-head. They always caught bullheads, and it was very tricky to remove those from the hook. The sharp horns on the sides of their heads caused a lot of pain if they stuck the person trying to free them, so Grampa Jim usually removed them from the hook.

Cleaning those rascals was a trick, too. It took a few lessons to learn how to avoid getting hurt by their horns. After the fish were cleaned outdoors, Kate took the catch to the house to wash them and get them ready for frying. Later, we all enjoyed a delicious bull-head dinner, with the fish fried in butter, along with fresh lettuce salad and veggies from the garden. Dessert was usually ice cream with fresh strawberries on top. Jim never ate a meal without some kind of dessert to finish.

Grampa Jim owned two ponies. He got them for the grandchildren to ride but they were rather mean. They had the disposition of Shetland ponies but they were much larger. They would only run when they were returning home from an excursion and then the kids couldn't stop them until they were in the barn. The other ornery deed they did was to rub up against a fence so that the rider's legs would get scratched or cut. They turned out to be more unpleasant to deal with than fun, but all the children remember them because of their disagreeable personalities.

Rick remembers a time when he fell off Brownie because Brownie was misbehaving, and vowed he would never get on him again. Kate and I persuaded him to change his mind and to show Brownie who was boss. Rick was very reluctant to remount Brownie but he did, and successfully handled the pony the rest of the afternoon. It was another "stay in the buggy" lesson.

Rick tells about a time when Merrill's children were still living on the farm. Cousins Rhonda and Rick, both about four years old, thought it would be fun to throw eggs against the side of the chicken house. They introduced this game to their younger siblings as well. The children had great fun throwing the eggs and watching them splatter. Later, when Gramma Kate returned and went to the chicken house to gather eggs, strangely, there were no eggs. She figured out what had happened when she saw the side of the chicken house and the shells. She was quite angry and made them clean up the mess. She scolded them and instructed them to never do that again. They clearly got her message but both still remember the fun they had watching them splatter!

A story that frequently gets told is the time no one could find shoes for the twins Brad and Barry. All four Cranston children were staying at the farm with Gramma Kate and Grampa Jim. It was Sunday morning. They all knew Gramma and Grampa went to church on Sunday morning. Everyone was getting dressed in their Sunday clothes but no one could find shoes for the twins. Everyone was searching except Brad and Barry. They were sure that if no one could find their shoes they would not have to go to church.

The searchers looked everywhere—upstairs and downstairs, under the beds, in all the rooms, and even outside the house. The shoes were nowhere to be found. Brad and Barry, at age five, seemed completely calm about not finding their shoes, sort of "ho-hum" about the whole thing. There wasn't much time left to look, as they had to allow time to travel—the church was twelve miles away. They also needed to pick up some other children on the way. Finally, Gramma Kate said, "They don't need their shoes. They can just go barefoot." Carole and Rick were mortified to think that they were taking the twins to church barefoot, but Gramma was determined they would not miss church. She loaded them in the car, even though they were a bit late. Oddly, when they got home, Brad and Barry found their shoes and never tried to outmaneuver Gramma Kate again.

When we lived in Willow Lake, camping was becoming a popular activity. Our family purchased a self-contained camper which slept six people and could easily increase that to eight. It was twenty-three feet long with a kitchen, a bathroom, and an upper bunk that slept two. Our family lived in it while Jack and I attended summer school at Northern State College in Aberdeen. Later we used it for many family camping trips. Kate and Jim loved to go camping with us and we made several trips to Montana and Washington to visit the Merrill Gunderson family and other relatives.

When we parked for the night Kate, the social butterfly, took a walk to introduce herself to our neighbor campers and have a chat with them. She wanted to know where everyone was from. She made sure we had hamburger and steak to feed the family, and prepared dinners fit for royalty. Jack always did the grilling but she fixed the other dishes and made sure we were all well fed. My family often reflects, with amusement, on our camping trips with Gramma Kate enthusiastically participating.

A Tribute to Grandma Kate

By Brianne Cranston-Miller, Kate's granddaughter, written in 2002 while attending college at Colorado State University at Ft. Collins

She is beautiful. Her smile has always contagiously filled each room she wandered into. She is a teacher, a poet, an artist, and a jump roper. She is a mother, a daughter, a grandmother and a great-grandmother. She is a wife, a chef, a quilter and a sister. She is a musician, a mentor, and most importantly, an inspiration.

As a young girl growing up in a world filled with stereotypes and barriers, I had encouragement from many amazing people throughout the years. There is, however, a very important woman who has, and always will, play a significant role in the person I am and will become. This woman is my Great Grandma Kate. At ninety-five years old, I've never before had the amazing privilege of knowing a more enthusiastic, active, and loving person. Her active take on life is never-ending. She is always up to play games with the great-grandkids. I remember believing, as a little girl, that if I were lucky enough to grow up and be anything like her and have grandkids loving me like we loved her, then life would be good.

I still think one of the most amazing memories I have as a child took place when I was about eight years old and Grandma was around eighty-five. My dad tells it best. He always begins with a hearty laugh and a big grin. He continues laughing and says, "I heard a lot of commotion outside, lots of laughing and loud clicking sounds. I still remember walking to the window and watching in awe as my grandma jumped rope with my daughter. I couldn't believe it." Of course, back then I wasn't old enough to hold a true appreciation for the things she did and the sacrifices she made, but as a young child I'm not sure she could have done anything much cooler than jumping rope with me that day. From that day forward, I've looked up to her as more than a great grandma. The older I've gotten the more I look forward to her stories of when she was a girl, growing up in some of the most devastating times America suffered through.

I mean, not only was she a cool grandma, but she was a picture of courage and confidence for me to gaze at. After finally grasping the significance of what it meant to survive World War I and World War II, the Great Depression, the Vietnam War, and more recently, the terrorism scare, I had a small, but important understanding of what it had been like to be my grandma. She had gone from teaching in a one-room school house in South Dakota to taking the World Wide Web by storm—she's an e-mail fanatic. I realize that we may all have to eventually take changes similar to these in stride as we grow older, but I can only pray that I am strong enough to face them with as much courage as Kate Gunderson.

Grandma Kate, as she is referred to affectionately by both grand-kids and great-grandkids, hasn't adopted the label of inspiration for just any reason. After hearing stories about both my grandma and her brother, and my dad and his siblings, I can only imagine the patience Grandma Kate must have exerted over the years. That alone deserves an award. More than this, I admire her for her beautiful piano playing and vocal abilities. I admire her for her intricately detailed quilts that have kept me warm over the years. I admire her for her astounding memory; she's never forgotten a birthday.

With her passion for life, she's inspired me to be to be successful by impacting an individual's life—not with money, or fame, or empty promises, but by showing them the beauty the world holds for them.

FORTY-ONE

Kate the Caregiver

As the oldest daughter in her family, Kate was given more responsibility. She helped with the housekeeping duties and also with caring for younger siblings. Her siblings saw her as the person to go to when they needed to be consoled, or entertained. She helped with their emotional hurts and their physical wounds. She guided them in making decisions and solving their problems. Anna depended on Kate to be there for her, also, and it is my belief that when Kate left home for her education, Anna grieved her loss. This separation was hard for Anna, Charlie, and the rest of the children. But Charlie recognized Kate's strength and independence as a special gift and he was determined she would learn how to share it with the world. He may have had a premonition that the family would need her strength one day.

Things began to happen in 1934. Charlie was doing carpenter work away from home one day when he suffered a serious heart attack. He was rushed to the local doctor and sent on to the closest hospital in Mitchell, SD. Emil, Lena and Bill were the only children still living at home with Charlie and Anna.

Lena shared some of her thoughts of that time:

"I think I was 10 or 11 years old and I remember someone came to our school to get Emil, Bill, and me. We were told our dad was seriously ill, in the hospital, and we were taken to Mitchell to be with other family members. When we arrived at the hospital we were taken to Dad's room and it was obvious he was in terrible pain and struggling to breathe. He was told we were there and then we were taken to the hallway where we sat waiting for Jennie (Henry's wife) to pick us up to take us to her mother's home in Mitchell. We stayed with her until our father died."

The older siblings remained at the hospital until Charlie's death two days later. Charlie was sixty-three years of age and left a wife and three children at home.

Arrangements were made for the funeral and burial, but that was only the beginning. What was Anna going to do now? Could they stay on the farm? Who would do the farm work? What did the future hold? There were more questions than answers.

It was decided among the siblings that, for now, the family would remain on the farm. Emil, age 17, would continue to do the farm work, and Bill, age 13, would help. It was the end of February and Emil planned to drop out of school to make sure the planting got done in the spring. The older boys—Henry, Fred and Ira—could also pitch in when necessary. Jim could help sometimes, too. Kate began to make plans to help in other ways. She knew they all also needed a lot of emotional support.

It soon became obvious that the family could not remain on the farm. They had survived but living conditions were challenging and selling the farm was the sensible thing to do. When Bill graduated from high school, and Lena was going into twelfth grade, Anna accepted an offer to be housemother for two of the Kleppin boys from the Wessington Springs area who had enrolled in college at South Dakota State College in Brookings. The Kleppins rented a house in Brookings where the boys could live while attending college. It sounded like an ideal arrangement for Anna, Bill and Lena. Bill could attend college classes and Lena could finish high school in Brookings. Anna kept house for all of them, and the Kleppins helped pay expenses plus a fee for Anna's work. Emil struck out on his own, getting a job on another farm. The plan worked well until Lena graduated—then all the boys were drafted into the army to serve during WWII. Anna was informed that a rancher in the Chamberlain area was looking for a housekeeper. She inquired about the job and was hired. She moved there alone.

Lena enrolled in college at General Beadle State Teachers College in Madison, SD. Her sister Mary was married to Elmer Gerth and they lived on a farm near Estelline, which is not far from Madison. Mary and Elmer helped Lena find a place where she could work for her room and board while attending college. Mary and Kate loaned Lena clothing from their closets. She also received money and advice from both sisters about a variety of matters relating to growing up—even if she didn't ask for it. Years later Lena thanked Kate, through her laughter, for the advice she had given, and admitted she had needed it.

Emil and Bill both lived with Kate and Jim and at the Henry Wilson home periodically for their home base after they left the farm. Both boys were involved in serious military battles while in the army. Emil saw action in Europe and Bill served for four years in Guam, Okinawa, and other islands in that area. When Bill returned to the US he was extremely stressed. He suffered from PTSD, called "shell-shock" in those days. He paced the floor and was a chain smoker. He didn't talk, and Merrill and I were told not to bother him. Kate knew he needed time to heal—not from physical wounds, although he had some of those—but emotionally. I was young, maybe nine or ten, and didn't pay much attention to grownup matters so I really don't know how long he stayed with us. When he wanted to talk, Kate sat down and listened to him, and she invited him to stay as long as he wished. He began to have brief conversations with her—not about the war, but about his future. Kate encouraged him to attend church with us, and choir rehearsals too. The people in the Salem Church community were good for him, and before long he became interested in one of the girls in the choir. Bill and Darlene Peterson married in 1950.

Years went by and more changes took place in the family. Some relocated and established homes in other places, but for Anna it was always a problem of where to have her own home. She and Lena were living in Wessington Springs, where Lena taught school, but Lena decided to move to the state of Washington to teach. After selling their house in Springs, Anna was invited to spend a period of time with each of the children every year instead of purchasing a home.

When cancer reared its ugly head the second time for Anna, not even surgery could stop it.

Kate said, "My home is your forever home. Please stay here."

Anna drew her last breath in Kate and Jim's bedroom on their farm. Both of them, and other family members, cared for Anna there until the end of her life in 1962.

Charlie Wilson family about 1924. Back L-R: Fred, Ira, Kate. Middle L-R: Henry's wife Jenny, Henry, Anna, Mary, Charlie, Charlotte. Front L-R: Emil, Bill, Lena.

Charlie Wilson family with spouses at Bill Wilson's wedding, 1950. Back L-R: Jim Gunderson (Kate), Henry Wilson (Jenny), Ira Wilson (Lois), Marvin Erickson (Charlotte), Fred Wilson (Lillian), Elmer Gerth (Mary). Middle L-R: Kate Gunderson (Jim), Jenny Wilson (Henry), Charlotte Erickson (Marvin), Lillian Wilson (Fred), Bride Darlene Wilson (Bill), Groom Bill Wilson, Gary Gerth (Elmer). Front L-R: Lena Lunnum (Arnold), Lois Wilson (Ira). Seated: Anna Wilson, mother of Groom (father Charlie was deceased). Not pictured: Emil Wilson (Marie).

Kate the Animal Lover

KATE LOVED ANIMALS, both large and small, and she taught me to respect and love them. She liked helping with daily outside chores and was always very kind to the animals.

I remember taking baby kittens into the house and feeding them milk. Sometimes I dressed them in my doll clothes. We always had a dog, but it wasn't until I was nearly ten years old that I was allowed to have a dog that lived in the house. Kate bought me a rat terrier puppy and I practically smothered her with love. I wanted to have her on my lap when I ate and wanted her to sleep on my bed at night. I had to go to school without her but the minute I got home I had her on my lap. We were inseparable.

Wessington Springs did not run school buses when my brother started high school there. He chose to commute with some other boys who drove into town daily. They picked him up each morning at the end of our driveway. One morning the puppy followed him, and he didn't notice her. The driver of the car didn't see her either, until it was too late, and he ran over her.

The loss of the puppy was very difficult for me and Merrill apologized many times. He, too, was sad. My parents tried to console me, promising they would look for another puppy. They were true to their word and about a year later they bought another rat terrier puppy for me.

We named the puppy Lucky. The owners said the puppies would be destroyed if they didn't find homes for them, so this little guy was pretty lucky. I loved Lucky like I had loved my first puppy. He was my constant companion when I was home.

One summer day, as Lucky and I were walking around in the trees behind our house, he spotted a cat and began to chase it. The cat went up a low hanging branch and Lucky followed, not noticing that he was going up a tree. When he found himself up high he was afraid to come down, and whined and cried. I knew I could climb up to rescue him, but before I reached him he became so nervous and scared that he jumped down, a distance of about six or eight feet. He injured his hind legs and couldn't walk. I was in a panic to help him so I picked him up, which was probably the wrong thing to do. I got him to the house. Kate examined him and decided we should take him to the animal doctor in town.

The veterinarian said Lucky had an injury that he couldn't fix and suggested that we "put him down." I just couldn't agree to do that, so we took him home. Kate made a wonderful bed for him and we fed and watered him, and carried him outside for bathroom duties all summer. I was starting high school that fall and would be staying in town all week and coming home on week-ends. My mother and dad assured me that they would care for Lucky during the weekdays. Kate was teaching school during the day and, surprisingly, Jim said he would care for the dog during the day until she got home from school. He seemed to be buying into the dog project, too.

Kate had started her own version of therapy for the dog by this time, and a couple of times a day she helped Lucky do walking exercises. She supported him while moving his legs, and she massaged his back and legs with tender loving care. Soon Lucky began to respond by moving his legs, and after a while he could take a step. Kate could see that her therapy was helping and the whole process became a challenge to her. She was determined to help the dog regain his ability to walk.

Her care, with my dad's help, was really starting to pay off. Lucky began to take steps. Even though his hind legs had atrophied somewhat because he hadn't used them, he was getting some strength in them. He was slightly deformed but he actually started to walk again. He wasn't running but he could walk around the house and the yard. I know Lucky wouldn't have walked again without Kate's loving care and determination to make it happen. Lucky lived a fairly normal life for several more years with Jim and Kate, and was quite mobile. What a lucky dog!! He was appropriately named.

Fast forward a generation, many years later. My daughter Carole seemed to have a special gift for communicating with her pets and they responded to her love for them. She graduated from high school and was living in Huron when she was introduced to a litter of miniature husky puppies and fell in love with them. She bought one but was later told she could not have a puppy in her apartment. Carole didn't want to give up this beautiful puppy but was having problems finding a place for him to live.

As a last resort, she approached her brother Brad, who was living in the basement of Grandma Cranston's house, begging him to sneak the dog in temporarily while she decided what to do with him.

"Sure," Brad said, "I can take him in the outside entrance to the basement. Grandma doesn't use that entrance much and seldom goes downstairs these days. I think we can do that." The arrangement worked for a couple weeks until one day Grandma Cranston heard a dog barking and went to investigate. She informed Brad he could not have the dog in the apartment and he should find a different home for him.

There was only one thing to do—call Gramma Kate. They were

sure she would love to own Jacque. They thought if she saw him she wouldn't be able to say no.

A trip to Wessington Springs was planned with the puppy. They were right—Gramma Kate and Grampa Jim both fell in love with the puppy. Jacque had a forever home with them. Jacque went everywhere with Grandpa Jim and he took long walks with Kate in the country. He grew into an exceedingly happy and beautiful dog. When they moved into town he adjusted to his new surroundings, and after Jim passed away he and Kate became even closer. Jacque turned out to be the best companion she could have asked for.

FORTY-THREE

Farming Partners

MY BROTHER MERRILL married Dakota Knigge in 1954. At first, they rented farms near my parents' farm, but a few years later, Merrill and Dakota and Jim and Kate agreed to farm together, and another house was moved to the Gunderson farm for Merrill and his family. Living on the same farm was a lot more convenient, especially since they shared a lot of the same machinery.

Kate often spoke of how much she enjoyed Merrill and Dakota's children as they grew up. Their house was not even a block from Kate and Jim so the grandchildren were with Kate many times each day. They did a lot of things together. Dakota became my mother's deputy at the Office of Treasurer of Jerauld County. They commuted to town together and worked together.

Merrill and Dakota lived on the same farm with my parents for several years, but the farm wasn't quite large enough to support two families and eventually Merrill and Dakota and their children Rhonda, Randy, and Dana, moved to Michigan, where my first cousin Don Wilson and his family lived. Merrill worked for a logging company. His and Dakota's fourth child, Sonja, was born there.

Work circumstances and life experiences later led Merrill to seek logging employment in the Montana mountains. Later still, they ended up renting several thousand acres of land in Washington state where Merrill became a successful dry land wheat farmer until he retired. Dakota was manager of a retirement home in Ephrata for many years.

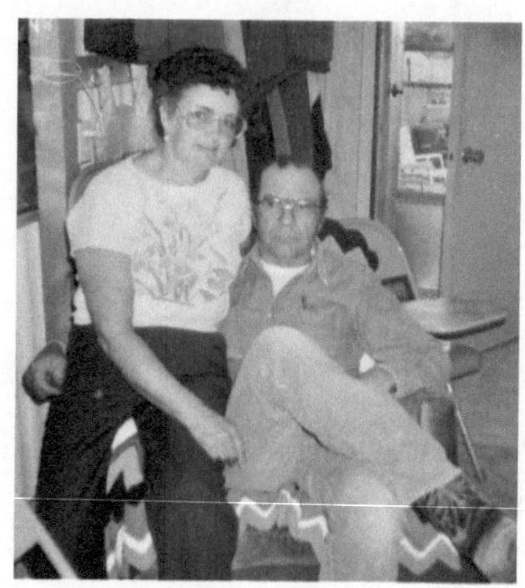

Merrill and Dakota around 1970

My brother Merrill Gunderson passed away in 2010 and his wife, Dakota Knigge Gunderson, passed away in 2020.

FORTY-FOUR

Life in Town

JIM AND KATE remained on the farm after Merrill and his family moved. A few years later Jim was experiencing heart problems, and he and Kate wanted to be located near a doctor. They decided to check the housing availability in Wessington Springs.

They found a delightful two bedroom home very close to downtown. They concluded they would live there in the winter and go back to their farm home during the summer. Jim no longer owned any livestock and didn't do any farming. He rented his farm ground to his nephew.

They planted a big garden on the farm and just maintained the yard during the summer. It was very pleasant to live in the country all summer in their old home. They planned to rent the city home to Kate's sister-in-law Jennie during the summer.

It soon became apparent to Kate that Jennie was trying to help her son Don and his wife Joyce. They had all returned to the Springs area. Don was in a wheelchair. Kate recognized Don and Joyce needed a place to live. Kate and Jim sold them their house at a reduced price, and my parents went house hunting again.

Jim and Kate found a home to buy on the other side of town

and moved there. Kate had the kitchen remodeled and they made some other improvements. Jim was really happy to have a garage for their car. In all the years they were married they had never had a decent garage; now they had a large steel building that would shelter the car and store other machines, like a mower.

They were living there when Jim passed away in 1989. Kate decided to keep her residence there.

She continued to live a busy, purposeful life after Jim's death. She missed Jim but she had things to do and stayed busy in the community. She was involved in church activities, such as sewing quilt tops and helping the ladies tie quilts; she helped with all the church dinners; and she attended Bible studies. She met her friends at the local senior center to have lunches and also volunteered her time there. She read and recorded many books for the blind for the South Dakota State Library. Through a connection with a pastor who started a prison ministry, she became a pen pal with prisoners in a federal prison. Her home became a place where nieces and nephews could stay temporarily as they attended high school classes in Springs if they could not get home because of bad weather, or if they had an evening school activity. She even volunteered to tutor them if they needed help with homework. She searched for good used clothing for children in an orphanage that she supported in India. Kate and her friends attended school and community events and they traveled, taking several bus tours together.

Kate spent a lot of time with her sister-in-law Jennie doing puzzles and playing board games. Jennie lived alone and was mostly homebound.

Still, Kate *made* time to send birthday greetings to all her relatives as well as many friends, always with a hand-written note sending her love and blessings.

Kate lived alone for several years in Wessington Springs in the house that she and Jim had bought. One day an old friend from Kimball contacted her and asked her to go out for coffee with him.

Bill Larsen was an acquaintance from her youth, and she remembered going on a few dates with him. A friend of hers from grade school had been married to him for many years. Bill told her his wife Anna had died and he was lonely.

Kate and Bill Larsen

Kate was not lonely but she did feel an attraction to Bill. He kept coming back to see her and one day asked her to marry him. He was eighty-six years old and Kate was eighty-five. She was not sure it was wise to marry at their age. She was impressed with Bill's family. She found them friendly, conversational, and accepting of her being with Bill. After discussing it for several months Bill and Kate decided to go ahead with their marriage.

They had a private ceremony at Our Savior's Lutheran Church in Wessington Springs. Kate's brother Bill and his wife Darlene were their attendants. They had no guests for the ceremony but they had dinner afterwards with relatives from both sides of the family. ˙

FORTY-FIVE

New Family with Bill

BILL AND KATE decided to live in Bill's home located between Kimball and Gann Valley, near his sons Rod and Steve. Bill had a beautiful ranch style house which he had recently built, near Kate's original home in Buffalo County. Kate remembered some of his neighbors. It was an unusual coincidence that she ended up living near the same neighborhood in which she had grown up.

Bill Larsen family members: L-R Dallas, Vivian, Steve, Bill, Rod

Bill's family was younger than Kate's, and his grandchildren were still attending school. His children and grandchildren were all very accepting of Kate and affectionate with her. He had four children, all married with families. Two sons, Rod and Steve, lived with their families near Bill in the Kimball area. Son Dallas and family lived near Scottsbluff, NE. His only daughter was a widow who lived in Bison, SD with her daughter. Coincidentally, Kate was well acquainted with one of the mothers-in-law.

Kate kept her home in Wessington Springs, and she and Bill continued to attend church there part of the time and visited Kate's relatives and friends some weekends. It was a big adjustment for Kate to make the move to Kimball, but making regular visits back to Wessington Springs made it easier. She decided to sell the family farm outside Wessington Springs.

When Bill became ill early in 2000, his doctor recommended that they live in an assisted living facility in Chamberlain, located on the banks of the Missouri River. They rented a beautiful two bedroom apartment with all the amenities one could ever want. Bill's family visited frequently, and Jack and I tried to get there every two weeks from Huron, a distance of ninety miles. Kate loved living there. She was busy all the time and enjoyed visiting with the other residents. She joined them in exercise class, doing puzzles, worship services (for which she played piano), and she especially loved the meals that were served in a beautiful common dining room for all the residents.

Since Kate was very social, this style of living suited her very well. Her next door neighbor was losing her sight and Kate spent hours reading books to her. Since she had recorded books for the blind for the South Dakota State Library for many years, reading to her neighbor was nothing but fun for her.

Kate's health was becoming somewhat challenging during this time. She had osteoporosis, causing her to have a deformed back. She also suffered an appendicitis attack at age ninety-one, which required an ambulance transport to Mitchell from Chamberlain to receive an emergency appendectomy. She survived the operation and was released from the hospital to stay at my house for two weeks in Huron to recuperate.

Sometime later, Kate fell in their apartment at the assisted living facility. She broke a pubic bone, causing excruciating pain and misery for many months. During that time she was in the Huron Regional Hospital and Sunquest Nursing Home in Huron. I seriously thought she would not survive, but slowly she improved after hospitalization and a long period of recuperation in the nursing home. She was dismissed on the condition she stay in Huron at my home for a period of time. The doctor wanted her nearby as she continued to convalesce.

Kate became well enough to return to the facility in Chamberlain, but not long after that Bill became seriously ill and passed away. My husband had recently died, and I was living alone at that time, so I invited Kate to come live with me permanently in Huron. After taking some time to think about it she accepted my invitation and moved to Huron in February of 2004.

Shortly after Kate moved to Huron we decided to look for another home in Huron. We looked at a lovely one located just south of the city limits. It was somewhat larger than my current home and we liked the rural flavor of country living. We made an offer on it and the seller accepted.

Gayle, Kate, & Merrill around 2004

Kate had a cute little room with plenty of sunshine. It was close to the bathroom, kitchen and the other bedroom where I would be sleeping. She had lots of room for shelves on which to place her many pictures; a single bed; and a small rocking chair with a matching ottoman. The room had a large closet, and large windows on the east and the south so she got plenty of sunshine. There was room to put a small desk. The bathroom was conveniently located just across the hallway, only a few steps from her door. She had all the space she needed and it was bright and cheery.

Our new house was very comfortable and convenient. She did have to adjust to a lot less activity. This was quiet living compared to the assisting living facility, but I tried to get her involved in my church. My daughter Carole dropped in frequently, and sometimes the grandchildren visited, but it was still not as social as the assisted living center.

She read a lot of books and wrote many letters until her eyesight failed. Then we got her interested in listening to audio books which we ordered weekly from the SD State Library. She loved listening to the books and they became her main entertainment. It was also convenient, as the books arrived by mail.

Best friends! Kate with two more dogs, Taffy and Chino

My daughter Carole heard about someone who bought a bischon-poo designer dog—a cross between a bischon and a poodle. Seeing it in a picture, we thought that Kate would like a dog for a companion while I was helping at the Coffee Tree, an eatery my daughter and I owned in downtown Huron. We called the breeder in Minnesota and they had a puppy available. We asked them to save her for us and we would pick her up. Carole and I loaded Kate into my car and left immediately. We all fell in love with the puppy the minute we saw her. She sat on Kate's lap all the way home and never left her side again unless she was outside to potty, or if I took her for a walk. We named her Taffy and she brought Kate much joy. Taffy had a laid back personality and was very smart. We easily trained her and she was a perfect companion for Kate. They sat together all day long every day in Kate's chair in her room, or shared a chair in the living room.

Later I purchased a little poodle to join us. We named her Cappuccino, because that was the color her fur was supposed to be as an adult, just as Taffy was supposed to be the color of taffy candy. When the poodle's fur didn't change color we shortened her name to Chino. The two puppies became attached at the hips. They did everything together, and Kate and I spoiled them profusely. The dogs loved Kate so much that they rarely left her side. She accommodated them and fed them treats often, even from the table.

Time passed quickly and when Kate was approaching her ninety-eighth birthday we decided we should have a special celebration. We invited all the Larsen families and some of Kate's close friends. We also rented a limousine to pick her up for a ride around Huron because she had never ridden in a limousine.

My son and family came from Denver to help with the party. Rick and Kristi are both very creative and cleverly decorated the house appropriately. We converted the house into a nice restaurant, and set up tables for the meal. We prepared a dinner of BBQ ribs, baked potatoes, and vegetable salad. Of course, we had a special cake baked in her honor and she received a beautiful bouquet of flowers.

Every effort was made to make the birthday party a memorable celebration. Kate was radiant. She looked beautiful and celebrated with great gusto.

Kate at her 98th birthday party

One Last Hurrah

ONE OF THE most memorable adventures that my daughter Carole and I ever experienced was when we accompanied Kate to Seattle to see her youngest and only surviving sibling, Lena.

Carole and I owned and operated a coffee house in downtown Huron. We saw an announcement for a convention in Seattle for owners and/or employees of coffee houses. It would be good for us, as owners, to attend such a convention, and we could take Kate with us. She could stay with her sister Lena and husband Arnold, who lived near Seattle, at Stanwood, WA. We thought the sisters might not have another chance to see each other since Kate was in her late nineties. This could be a great opportunity for all of us. When we asked Kate about it she was a little hesitant, but after some thought she decided to go.

We purchased plane tickets to travel from Minneapolis because it would be a direct flight—no layover and we wouldn't need to change planes. We made a plan to drive to Minneapolis and stay overnight in a motel near the airport because our flight was scheduled to leave early in the morning. We received permission from the motel to leave our car there for the duration of the trip and we could take the shuttle from the motel to the airport early the next morning.

The travel agent informed us that since Kate didn't have a valid driver's license she would not need to show it at the airport, but she would need a picture ID. The agent suggested we have her picture taken in Brookings at the driver's exam station on our way to Minneapolis. Kate could use that picture to present at the airport in order to check in.

On the day we were to depart, we left home in Huron about 1:00 p.m. and drove to Brookings. When we arrived and requested a picture they said they couldn't do that without a birth certificate from Kate. A birth certificate for Kate did not exist! We offered other sources of ID but they would not consider taking the picture without her birth certificate. We had a family conference and decided to call Pierre to see if they had a record of her birth. Feeling totally helpless, I said, "But my mother was not born in South Dakota. She was born in Omaha, Nebraska!" Carole, feeling both frantic and frustrated, asked, "Can you call somewhere in Omaha?" Kate and I were desperately trying to determine where we could call.

The employees at the transportation office were not interested in helping us. In fact, they seemed to be enjoying our struggle. They offered no suggestions or options at all. We had a real dilemma—and the office would close at 5 p.m.

After much thought and kicking around ideas about what to do, a thought came to me. I vaguely remembered having seen Kate's old driver's license in her room in a drawer at home. We asked the people at the office if they would accept it as proof of Kate's identity. Miraculously, they said they would.

I called my son Brad at work and briefly explained our dilemma. "Could you go to the house and see if you can find Gramma Kate's old driver's license? I think it is in an old wallet in her dresser, in the top right-hand drawer. I need you to bring it here. We have to present it to the agents by 5 p.m. in order to get her picture taken for ID at the airport."

He replied, "Okay, I'll go and look. Will they hold the office open a few minutes if I don't make it by 5?"

I asked. They said no.

"Let's do this," I said. "You get her license and start driving here. We will leave here and drive until we meet you somewhere between Arlington and De Smet. Never mind the speed limit. I will pay all fines."

We quickly got in our car and drove nearly 90 mph. We met Brad between Arlington and De Smet, as I expected we would, and he handed off the driver's license to Carole through the window. We turned around on the road and raced back to Brookings. We had just enough time for Kate to have her picture taken and a she had a new ID in her hand before they closed the office. We all breathed a sigh of relief, waved a thank you, thanked God, and calmly proceeded to travel on to Minneapolis.

We arrived in Minneapolis after dark. With no GPS at that time, we were fumbling with the map, trying to find the motel. After several attempts leaving the main interstate highway, we found ourselves continually returning to the same spot, to try all over again. Finally we stopped at a gas station to get directions, and soon arrived at the motel and got checked in. We had a clean, comfortable room. We would rise early, because the shuttle left for the airport at 8:30 a.m. All of us slept well thinking things were now under control.

Carole went downstairs the following morning to get coffee for us while I repacked our suitcases, and then she went to check us out. A few minutes later she burst through the door exclaiming, "You guys! We have to be ready earlier than we thought! The shuttle will be here by 8:00 a.m. instead of 8:30. Throw that stuff in the suit cases NOW! We can't be late; they won't wait."

Getting a 98-year-old lady prepared for plane travel in a motel in Minneapolis in 15 minutes was a daunting assignment. We got everything in the suitcase and threw on some clothes and makeup. Kate's walker had a place to sit as well as to use for walking. When we got her positioned on the seat of her walker, Carole grabbed our luggage and ran down to the shuttle to try to hold them there while she made the case for them to "wait for my elderly grandmother to get on board!" I loaded the remaining luggage on the walker and as I moved Kate out of the motel room I said, "Okay, Mom, I want you to hold onto this walker with both hands. DO NOT LET GO!! I'm going to run down this hallway"—which appeared to be the longest hallway I had ever seen—"to the elevator. When we get off the elevator I will be running part of the time, too. Just hang on tight!"

She replied, "Okay, I'm ready."

I ran, pushing the walker ahead of me with her seated on it, her hair flying back from the wind we created. We didn't have to wait for the elevator. We got on, arrived on the first floor and I pushed her outside then I ran again to reach the shuttle. Carole met me to help Gramma Kate get in the vehicle. The driver even gave her some assistance.

Suddenly I realized we could not take the walker with us on the shuttle or on the airplane. I ran, pulling the walker behind me, bumping and rolling, bouncing crazily, to our car in the parking lot. I unlocked the car, threw the walker in the back seat, locked the car and ran back to the shuttle. By then I was a mess, but we made it and were on our way to the airport. Whew!

We unloaded our luggage and entered the airport. Both of us helped Kate navigate to the counter to check in, check her baggage, and request assistance from the airport staff to provide transportation for Kate to our gate. When we arrived we found a comfortable place to sit and settled in to wait to board the plane.

We were feeling calm watching people when Kate figured out that one of the lenses of her glasses was missing. Earlier she had noticed that her eyesight seemed unusual but thought that one of the lenses was smeared and needed cleaning. When she discovered one of the lenses was missing she was immediately alarmed and very angry. She exclaimed, "I should not have tried to make this trip. This trip is a disaster, a mistake! I wish I could go home!"

Carole and I immediately analyzed what could have happened as we tried to calm Kate. What could we do? I called the motel and gave them a detailed report of our visit there and asked if they would please check in our room to see if they could find the lens. They were very courteous and kind and said that they would send someone to the room immediately.

Within fifteen minutes they returned our call and said they had found the lens and asked what they should do with it. I said I would pay the shipping charges if they would ship it overnight to Seattle. They told me they would be happy to ship it free of charge. Wow! I couldn't believe it! Our guardian angel was really busy that day!

Kate was surprised and pleased to hear I had been able to make these arrangements with the motel, as was I. We were amazed and relieved to be able to solve this complicated problem. Kate's eyesight had deteriorated severely, and it would be almost impossible for her to get along without her glasses.

When we arrived at the Seattle airport Lena and Arnold met us at the baggage claim area. It was a grand reunion. Watching Kate and Lena embrace and seeing the joy they experienced just seeing each other, made all the negative things we had experienced disappear. Carole and I decided it was worth everything we had gone through to get there.

We called and invited Kate's grandchildren in Ephrata (in central Washington) to come see Gramma Kate. Two families came to see us and we had a wonderful visit. The day after we arrived, the lens for Kate's eyeglasses was delivered to Lena's home, and we replaced it in her glasses. We thanked the Lord for another miracle.

Kate and Lena and Arnold had a fabulous visit, and Carole and I went on to attend our coffee convention. The remaining days of the trip were delightful, including a visit to see Duane—Lena and Arnold's son, and his wife, who live on the original property of the Lunnum family.

The return trip by air was smooth and uneventful, and we found it relaxing and enjoyable. When we walked into our home in Huron I commented, "Home sweet home."

Kate remarked, "It was worth all the fuss."

We all agreed, God is good!

Kate and Lena soon after our arrival in Stanwood WA. Lena was the youngest sister, Kate the oldest. This was the last time they saw each other. Lena was one of the first elementary school counselors hired in Seattle WA.

FORTY-SEVEN

Final Days

IN PREVIOUS YEARS when Carole and I needed a break from our ongoing, stressful responsibilities in Huron, we found Chandler, AZ a great place to visit. We thought Kate might like to celebrate her ninety-ninth birthday there with her sister Lena and her husband Arnold. When we contacted them they seemed excited to join us there so we spoke for a condo for two weeks in February of 2008. We knew the weather was pleasant in February and the condo was spacious and comfortable. Kate had been in wonderful health and we all looked forward to this trip.

On Sunday, at the beginning of our travel week, Kate was not feeling well, and on Monday she asked me to make an appointment to see Dr. Bob Hohm. When I was getting her ready to go Monday morning Taffy, our little bischon-poo, was very nervous about Kate leaving and wanted to go with us. I still remember how upset she was about us leaving home. She made more of a fuss than usual but I refused to take her with us.

The doctor thought everything was good but gave her a prescription for her heart rate. When we arrived home, an over-joyed Taffy met us at the door, happy to see Kate. She followed us into Kate's room and positioned herself next to Kate on her bed and stayed all day. Chino, our poodle, wanted to stay there also. They wouldn't even go out to potty without a lot of persuasion. The next day I had to pick them up and carry them outside because they didn't want to leave Kate. Their behavior was the same the following day. I thought they were acting very strangely and couldn't really understand it. Kate and I were amused and found their behavior humorous.

On Thursday Kate said she couldn't go on the trip. She wasn't feeling well enough and suggested that she go to the nursing home for two weeks and return home when Carole and I got back from Arizona. I decided that I would stay home too.

I had a hair appointment that day and a short time after I returned home Kate called me to her room. She was struggling to breathe. I found her condition so alarming that I called 911. I also called my son Brad to come home. He arrived in a few minutes and tried to help her. He gave her cardiac assistance until the ambulance arrived but by that time Kate was gone. The ambulance attendants urgently pressed me to decide whether or not to revive her. There were only seconds for a decision.

I had picked up Taffy and was in the doorway to Kate's room. Taffy was struggling to get away from me and return to the bed, to be near Kate. I had only seconds to make this life or death decision. My thoughts flashed back to the day Kate signed her living will in which she indicated that when it was time to go, she was ready. She had prayed to God several times during her previous illnesses, saying she was ready to give up her spirit to Him. She was one week from being ninety-nine years old and it did not seem reasonable to ask her to stay longer. It was very difficult, but I knew her wishes. I had to say no to resuscitation.

There is no way I can describe how hard that was, or how empty I felt as the ambulance crew left after offering their condolences. I put Taffy and Chino back on her bed and we all said our goodbyes to Gramma Kate. We huddled as close as we could get;

Taffy curled up around her head and Chino nestled next to her until the funeral director arrived to take her body to the funeral home.

The ambulance crew later told me it was wise not to try to revive Kate because they would have broken her ribs in the process and she would have suffered intense pain—and likely wouldn't have survived the process itself. At that time she was less than five feet tall and weighed under one-hundred pounds. She was so very small and physically feeble; yet to me she represented a dynamo of strength and a heart full of grace and love.

I was not aware then that the dogs had known Kate was near death. It was after her death I was told the dogs surmised Kate's condition. I find it fascinating—and touching—that they had a premonition her death was imminent, and were so devoted they didn't want to leave her side.

Kate Wilson Gunderson Larsen passed away on January 31, 2008 at age ninety-eight years and eleven months.

The funeral was held in Wessington Springs a few days later, after relatives from Washington arrived. She was buried beside my father, James Gunderson, in the cemetery at Salem Lutheran Church, where she had faithfully served years earlier in many capacities, and where my brother and wife—who have since died—are also buried.

Carole and I traveled to Chandler the following week to meet Lena and Arnold, who were already there. They had decided not to go to South Dakota for Kate's funeral since she had so recently visited them in Washington, with Carole and me. Lena wanted to remember those precious days they spent together in Washington. They had already been in Arizona for a week when Carole and I arrived one week late. We had a chance to talk about how Kate had spent her last days, which was comforting for all of us.

Carole and I did not know we would never see Arnold again. He passed away the following year. We did, however, travel to Washington to see Lena one more time. I felt I had a divine call—a tap on my shoulder—to spend a little more time with her. Carole graciously offered to travel with me again, and I am happy we saw Lena one last time. It was quality time and also included seeing my cousin Lonnie Gerth Mcbride, in Everett, WA—the only daughter of Mary Wilson Gerth (sister of Kate and Lena). Lena passed away the following year.

Kathryn Larsen

Kathryn Gunderson Larsen, 98, of Huron and formerly of Wessington Springs, died Thursday, Jan. 31, 2008, at her daughter's home.

The funeral will be at 1:30 p.m. Tuesday at Our Savior's Lutheran Church in Wessington Springs with the Rev. John Paulson officiating. Burial will be in Salem Lutheran Cemetery, rural Wessington Springs.

Kathryn Larsen

Friends may call Monday from 5 to 9 p.m., with a prayer service at 7 p.m., at the Basham Funeral Home in Wessington Springs and at the church Tuesday one hour prior to the service.

Kathryn Wilson was born Feb. 11, 1909, in Omaha, Neb., to Charles and Anna (Sick) Wilson. In 1927 She taught schools in Jerauld County for more than 30 years and was also Jerauld County treasurer for nine years.

She married James Gunderson in October 1929. They farmed in Jerauld County near Wessington Springs.

She married Bill Larsen in 1994. In February 2004 she moved to Huron to live with her daughter, Gayle Cranston.

She is survived by a son, Merrill (Dakota) Gunderson of Salome, Ariz.; a daughter, Gayle Cranston of Huron; a sister, Lena (Arnold) Lunnum of Standwood, Wash.; eight grandchildren, 16 great-grandchildren and two great-great-grandchildren.

She was preceded in death by her parents; her husbands; five brothers, Henry, Fred, Ira, Bill and Emil; two sisters, Mary and Charlotte; and a son-in-law, Jack Cranston.

As I write this book, there are now no surviving children from the family of Charles Philip Wilson and his wife Anna.

I pray the information in this book will be read, enjoyed, and shared for generations to come, and that it will serve as an inspiration to others to explore their roots and share their family stories.

"Be of good cheer. Do not think of today's failures, but of the success that may come tomorrow. You have set yourselves a difficult task, but you will succeed if you persevere, and you will find joy in overcoming obstacles. Remember, no effort that we make to attain something beautiful is ever lost." Helen Keller

FORTY-EIGHT

Legacy of Love

THE KATHRYN E. LARSEN ORPHANAGE

Over the years Kate received numerous letters in the mail requesting donations for charitable non-profit organizations. For several years she designated one day each month as her "gimme day"—her giving day. She carefully sifted through all the requests deciding which she would send a small donation. Not being wealthy, she couldn't afford large donations but was guided by the Bible verses in Matthew 25:35-36: *"For I was hungry and you gave me something to eat, I was thirsty and you gave me something to drink, I was a stranger and you invited me in, I needed clothes and you clothed me, I was in prison and you came to visit me."* Kate often remarked how blessed she felt to have a home, plenty of food, and sufficient clothing, and she wanted to share her blessings.

At church one Sunday in the early 1980s, a visiting pastor from a local church made an appeal for help with a project he had recently taken on. Pastor Einar Bach spoke about visiting an orphanage in India. He had never seen such poverty. The children slept on dirt floors. There was not enough food, and they dressed in ragged used clothing. He requested sponsors to make a monthly financial donation for individual orphans. Kate and a few others decided they would become sponsors, and not only send money but write letters of support to the children. She wanted to send words of encouragement and love.

After supporting orphans for two years, Pastor Bach reported he had accepted a call to become pastor at a church in Missouri. He issued a letter requesting someone to "please accept the responsibility of taking charge of the local sponsorship program." Kate volunteered. She felt it was a worthwhile project. She really wanted to make life better for the children at the orphanage.

Kate wrote letters to Pastor Zakkariah, the founder and director of the orphanage in India, and asked lots of questions. He replied, describing the conditions of extreme poverty, and especially the need for clothing for twenty-plus children ages of four to eighteen.

Kate swung into action, collecting used clothing. Some people gave her clothing, but she also shopped at rummage sales and the Salvation Army. She boxed the clothing and shipped it to the orphanage several times a year, paying shipping charges herself. She also sent "Pastor Z" extra money to help with other expenses —to help him buy a bike and a typewriter and a few other items he needed. She began making phone calls to him and became a prayer warrior for the orphanage. She also sent many letters of encouragement, reminding the pastor that God was watching and He would help. She promised to continue to pray for them.

She had been doing this for fifteen years or more when I became involved. Over the years other patronage had dwindled to nothing and Kate had become the sole supporter of the orphanage from the community of Wessington Springs, and very likely anywhere else.

Kate was growing older and changes were happening in her life. She had lost two husbands and was approaching the age of ninety-five when she moved to Huron, SD to live with me in 2004. She expressed her concern about what would happen to the orphanage when she was gone. Who would help Pastor Zakkariah?

I assured her that I certainly would continue to support the orphanage, but also suggested we search for additional means.

When we sent our most recent box of clothing, we were shocked to find the shipping expense had doubled. The category of shipping we previously used had been eliminated; now our only choice was shipping by air. This was not good. The cost of sending our last box exceeded the value of the contents! Kate and I faced a dilemma. How could we continue to help clothe the orphans?

We requested a meeting with the WELCA ladies (Women of the Evangelical Lutheran Church of America) of Our Savior's Lutheran Church in Huron where I am a member. We were looking for ways to support the orphanage. The ladies were agreeable and we discussed our problematic situation. Together we came to the conclusion that sending Pastor Zakkariah money was the most logical way to help them. Perhaps U.S. currency had more value there, and the pastor and his wife—who is his helper in the orphanage—could shop for children's clothing in India. The ladies made a small donation that day and said they would continue to donate in the future. We were thankful and appreciated having friends with whom we could talk.

While searching for other financial sources, Kate received a letter from Pastor Zakkariah informing her that the name of the orphanage was being changed to The K E Larsen Orphanage. Kate was very surprised to hear that news but also felt very honored. Our hearts were touched and the family celebrated over the new name of the orphanage.

A short time later the pastor informed us of the upcoming wedding of his son, Abraham Lincoln. In his letter he requested a nice business suit for Abraham to wear to his wedding. Kate and I had fun shopping for a suit we thought looked appropriate and about the right size for Abraham. My sons found a nice shirt and an attractive tie to go with the suit and, regardless of expense, we shipped the whole outfit to them. We felt pleased that the suit looked as though it fit Abraham nicely in the pictures of the wedding party we later received from Pastor Zakkariah.

The next year a baby girl arrived in the Zakkariah family. "Pastor Z" announced that his granddaughter's name was to be Kathryn Gayle. We were surprised, and in a telephone call to the pastor, Kate tried to persuade him to name the baby in honor of one of his relatives in India. They insisted on keeping the name, Kathryn Gayle, and again we felt very honored. With the help of the ladies from my church and our Pastor Katie, we got some special baptismal items together and sent them for little Kathryn Gayle's baptism.

We also established a penny offering for the benefit of the orphanage at Pastor Katie's suggestion. Each Sunday the children carry little buckets up and down the aisles, collecting loose change during the same time the regular offering is collected during the service. They take it to the front of the church and dump it into a large box with a window in it, so we can watch the money grow. At the end of each quarter the money is counted and that amount is wired to the orphanage in India. We are always amazed at the amount collected in loose change. Other times we have made the orphanage the recipient of funds from special fundraising events at our church.

Pastor Zakkariah and children in India

About two years after Kate's death, my son Rick—who lived and worked in Denver—received a phone call from his friend and previous co-worker Scott French. They had not talked for several years. Their conversation led to meeting over lunch the following week. As these old friends spoke about their present lives, Scott informed Rick that he had become passionately involved in a non-profit organization that helped orphans and abandoned children around the world. This faith-based organization was Global Hope, and he spoke about homes they had already established for orphans in Romania and Kenya.

Rick listened in amazement, and told Scott about his grandmother, Kate Larsen. He described her experience supporting an orphanage in India over the years, and inquired about the possibility of Global Hope connecting with them. Rick informed Scott that Kate was no longer alive, and that the family was now searching for additional sources of financial and spiritual support for the orphanage. Scott listened attentively, and indicated an interest. He wanted more information so I sent him some of Pastor Zakkariah's letters and pictures Kate had received.

Rick, his wife Kristi, their son Cory, and I attended the next annual dinner sponsored by Global Hope, where we heard about the orphanages they already sponsored. They also introduced the K E Larsen Orphanage as a prospective project, currently under prayerful consideration. We were very happy to hear them announce a plan to visit the orphanage in India to inspect the facility, and get acquainted with the director and his family to see if it would qualify for inclusion under the funding mechanism of Global Hope. That year Cory was graduating mid-year from Colorado State University. He decided to accompany the folks from Global Hope to India to visit the K E Larsen Orphanage.

The mission group included those knowledgeable about carpentry, plumbing, electricity, etc. When they arrived at the orphanage the need for all those things, and more, was obvious. They found extreme poverty and need.

They reported that the pastor and his wife and family had done an incredible job of caring for the twenty+ boys and girls living there, even though they lacked many essentials. They were impressed with the pastor and his wife, but it was obvious they needed a lot more help. Children lacked basics like clothing, food and medical attention—things many of us take for granted here. The children had no beds and slept on concrete floors. The toilet for the entire orphanage was an outhouse with a hole in the floor. There was no running water.

When the mission group arrived back in the U.S., they made recommendations to Global Hope regarding the great needs at the orphanage. They suggested constructing separate dormitories with bunk beds for the children. They also recommended running water, separate bathrooms and showers for boys and girls, improvements in electricity, and a refrigerator. They also needed a better concrete floor.

The mission team was impressed, however, that the orphanage was a place where love and joy flourished in the face of adversity. The pastor expressed a very strong faith which he passed along to the children. The children were resilient and happy, demonstrating a strong faith and instinct to survive, in spite of terrible hardship. The team shared how much their faith grew by witnessing the great faith of "Pastor Z" and his family.

Global Hope made plans to help this orphanage. My family was overjoyed to hear the good news. Global Hope would continue mission trips to make physical improvements at the orphanage, and to support the spiritual needs of the children.

During his time in India, my grandson Cory was impressed by the stories told by Pastor Zakkariah regarding Grandma Kate. "Pastor Z" had saved the letters he received from Kate. He brought them to Cory one day, and told him it was important for him to read them. He said, "There were times when I ran out of food, and

I had no money. I felt deeply discouraged and wanted to give up, close the orphanage. I thought I just couldn't go on another day. That was the day I would receive a letter of encouragement from Kate, which often contained a check. She told me how important my work was and encouraged me to continue. She said God would look on me with favor and would send more help. "Keep going, don't quit; stay in the buggy." God would hear my prayers. Kate said she and others were praying for us. The pastor expressed to Cory how grateful he was for Kate's financial support, the clothing she shipped, and her tenacity in prayer. He said he couldn't have survived without her support and encouragement.

Pastor Zakkariah, his wife, and their adopted daughter Jasmine have been dedicated workers in the orphanage. Their son Abraham and his wife have been an important part of caring for the orphans. They now have had another daughter, Kari Blessi, named in honor of one of the mission worker's daughters. It is possible that another of the pastor's sons, who is attending college, may also become involved in helping with the funding situation. His degree relates to marketing and fundraising.

Global Hope has recently begun to assist Abraham's mother-in-law in supporting a group of orphans in another location, as well as also establishing a home for boys in India.

Currently Global Hope is assisting Pastor Zakkariah with his efforts in community outreach by helping youngsters who don't live there but come to the orphanage daily for education and a free meal. Their mothers are most often involved in the sex trade because they have been abandoned by their husbands and have no other means to provide for their families. The mothers are uneducated, have no job skills, and are victims of abuse and desertion. Pastor Zakkariah also actively counsels approximately thirty lay pastors/gospel workers who have established small Christian congregations in the outlying areas. He has had an enormous Christian influence in that part of India.

Kate also deserves credit for "never giving up" in her prayers for the pastor and his mission in India. Her contributions might have been small but they were ever *so important* to Pastor Zakkariah.

Global Hope has been a real blessing to the K E Larsen Orphanage in India. Our Savior's Lutheran Church in Huron, SD still generously donates to the orphanage via Global Hope. Individuals have given as much as $500-$1000, which purchased bicycles for children who need to travel a distance for their school classes, and for other necessities. There are also other churches and individuals around the country who generously donate money and volunteer their skills and time.

I always hoped Kate would live to see the miracle for which she worked and prayed so many years. However, I believe God opened the door when the time was right. Never underestimate the results of ONE determined prayer warrior! God is always listening.

Kate never gave up. She could see the promised land even if she didn't experience it while she was alive. Her final mission, with the help of God, lives on and continues to grow!

Kate's final wish for the K E Larsen Home is *Stay in the Buggy*. A portion of proceeds from this book will be donated to the K E Larsen Home.

To make a direct donation go to www.globalhope.org and then look for India, and the K E Home for Orphans. There are also opportunities to sponsor children or become a Godparent.

To purchase this book or for more information contact the author here: Gcranstonauthor@gmail.com.

Gayle and her mother Kate

"In the battle of life it is not the critic who counts. Not the man who points out how the strong man stumbled or where the doer of deeds could have done better. The credit belongs to the man who is actually in the arena, whose face is marred by dust and sweat and blood; who strives valiantly; who errs and comes short again and again; who knows the great enthusiasms, the great devotions and spends himself in a worthy cause. Who, at the best, knows in the end the triumph of high achievement; and who, at the worst, if he fails, at least fails while daring greatly, so that his place shall never be with those cold and timid souls who know neither victory nor defeat."

Theodore Roosevelt

About the Author

This tribute to my mother was a lifelong goal and a labor of love. I hope you enjoyed it.

Gayle Cranston is a native of Wessington Springs, SD. A graduate of Huron College, she is a retired music teacher and former business owner who now resides in Huron, SD. She is active in Our Savior's Lutheran Church and the James River Writers group. The mother of four grown children, she proudly claims five grandchildren and seven great grandchildren. She lives with two strong-willed, pampered cats and one of her sons.

Stay in the Buggy is a personal story with historical anecdotes about Kate Wilson Gunderson Larsen and her family. Gayle is a first-time author and wrote this memoir in honor of her mother.

Acknowledgements

I appreciate the kind words of encouragement I received from a host of relatives and friends and others too numerous to mention to write a story about the life of my mother, Kate.

I would like to offer special thanks to Sallianne Hines, my editor, who provided me with the "rules of the road" in this project. Additionally, she encouraged me, advised me, listened to me, gave me creative ideas, and helped me over the finish line.

Margaret Schmidt contributed the buggy sketch used at chapter sections within the book, much thanks.

The James Valley Writers listened and advised me along the way, giving me encouragement to "Stay in the Buggy" until I finished the book.

My family, Rick and Kristi, Carole, Brad and Barry were cheerleaders for me and they generously shared their computer technology. Haley Cranston and Rick and Kristi Cranston were readers who shared ideas and suggestions.

Special thanks to Brianne Cranston-Miller, my granddaughter for her touching tribute to my mother and to Donna Thompson Steineke, Kate's former student, who also wrote a beautiful tribute.

Special friends who read the manuscript to offer their ideas and suggestions include, Jim and Barb Valer, Margaret Schmidt, Vikki Foley and her friend, Jeannette Kennedy, Scott French of Global Hope, Calvin O. Johnson, Molly Perry, Joan Kutter, Amanda Metzger, and Heidi Herman. Special thanks to Hazel Behrens and

Amanda Metzger for their help in setting up my Facebook author page.

A valuable source of information was the *Wilsonian Newsletter* which was circulated by two of my Wilson cousins, Fred and Daniel in the 1980's and 90's. Another cousin, Gary Gerth, also contributed more recent family history. I appreciated Fred and Gary reading my manuscript to make suggestions before publication.

Thank you to Pastor Zakkariah, founder and director of K E Larsen Home for Orphans in India, for his support and prayers.

My greatest gift was my mother, who never ran out of love for her family or friends. She was a great example of never, ever, giving up. My hope is that her story will inspire others to "Stay in the Buggy."

93-year-old Kate Larsen enters the world of computers

by Paulette Priebe

The computer world has a new fan. At 93 years of age, Kate Larsen of Chamberlain has taken up the computer and doing better than many who have been using one for years.

Kate started just three months ago using a laptop computer. But she found you can't send e-mail because there are no receiving towers in the area.

With some help by her daughter, Kate now has a desktop computer. She gets e-mails everyday from friends and relatives in Washington state, Michigan, Minnesota and Texas. She is now trying to get e-mail addresses of relatives living in Norway. She could become international.

"At first, I was nervous about making a mistake using it, but now I check my e-mails everyday," Kate said. "When we went on vacation, I came back to find 21 messages awaiting me."

She also uses the computer to gather information on different things.

Her daughter helped get Kate started, showing her how to run the computer. She has others helping her learn. Because Kate is a fast learner, she does not need much help now.

Kate's champion supporter is a lady she has known for over 50 years. She lives in Chicago and they e-mail each other very often.

"My life has gone around in a big circle," says Kate.

"I grew up in the Gann Valley area. It was in the days when it took my dad a whole day to get to Kimball with a team of horses pulling a wagon. These days, you just push a button and you get light, heat and mail!" says Kate. "With everything getting done so fast, you would think people had time to throw away. But they are busier than ever."

Starting high school at 13 in Springfield, Kate felt like a fish out of water. Their family sure did not get to town very often and she felt out of place.

The school was called Springfield Normal School. At this type of school in these days, if you attended all four years there, you could become a teacher upon graduation. There were 60 to 70 students enrolled. It was the last year for the school and everyone wanted to go there.

Kate's family moved on and she completed a year at Kimball High School. While in Kimball, she stayed there,

working to earn her keep.

Again, the family moved, this time Kate graduated from Gann Valley High School in 1927 in a class of eight. In Gann Valley, she stayed in town and had a job to pay her way also.

At 18, she began a 30-year teaching career. She taught in a rural country school in Jerauld County.

During this time, Kate took night classes and graduated from Huron College. It took longer than most, as she did it all at night.

After teaching, she tried her hand in politics. For eight years, Kate served as the Jerauld County Treasurer.

Next, she became an Avon lady. Her territory was rural Jerauld County.

Kate and her then husband of 60 years made their home in the Wessington Springs area.

After her husband died, Kate married Bill Larsen. He had lost his wife of 60 years also.

Bill's farm was about seven or eight miles from where she had grown up. This December, they will have been married eight years.

Kate has a daughter living in Huron and a son in the state of Washington. She has eight grandchildren and about 15 to 16 great-grandchildren. "I would have to stop and count them," she says.

One grandson, who lives in Denver, CO, works as a computer trouble-shooter.

The eldest grandson will be graduating soon from college and receiving his doctrine.

Besides working on the computer, Kate likes to crochet, embroider, read and play cards.

Bill and Kate now reside at

Regency Retirement Assisted Living Center in Chamberlain.

"This is the most perfect place. The only way it could be more perfect is if it were in Wessington Springs where all my old friends live," said Kate.

Highway patrol investigate lightning strike

by Paulette Priebe

Sergeant Larry Englund of the South Dakota Highway Patrol reported a motorcyclist was struck by lightning during a severe storm passing through Brule County on Aug. 8.

Around midnight, while driving on Interstate 90, near Mile Marker 291, James Calero of New Jersey was seriously injured by lightning.

A witness reported the incident to Highway Patrol Trooper Dan Bakke.

According to Trooper Bakke, after being struck, Calero flew from the motorcycle and landed in the median. The bike traveled through the median, across both westbound lanes and came to rest on the north side of the highway.

The motorcyclist was taken by White Lake Ambulance to Avera Queen of Peace Hospital in Mitchell.

Trooper Bakke reported the subject sustained burns and injuries on his upper body that were conducive to a person being hit by lightning.

Calero received severe head and face trauma from being thrown from the motorcycle. He was later transported to Sioux Falls.

Article originally printed in the Central Dakota Times, written by Paulette Prime, reprinted with permission.

SPIRIT OF DAKOTA

Award

September 29, 1989

Mrs. Kathryn Gunderson
510 N. State Avenue
Wessington Springs, SD 57382

Dear Kathryn:

    You have been honored as one of the nominees for
the annual Spirit of Dakota award which is an award honoring
an outstanding South Dakota woman in 1989.

    Although out of 52 nomination letters you were not
chosen as the winner this year, we do invite you (as a
nominee) to be our complimentary guest at the banquet,
SUNDAY, OCTOBER 29, at 5:00 PM at the Crossroads Hotel
and Convention Center in Huron. At this time, all nominees
will be especially recognized. In addition, there will
be a social and Dale Lamphere Art Show beginning at 4:00 PM.

    Our keynote speaker will be Betty Turner Asher,
the first woman president of a South Dakota university.
Prior to joining USD she was Vice-President of Student
Affairs at Arizona State University, the fifth largest
university in the nation. She received her doctorate
from the University of Cincinnati and has done postdoctorate
work at both Dartmouth and Harvard. The award will be
presented by the State's First Lady, Linda Mickelson.

    It is a great honor for you to have been nominated
and we know you must be very proud!

    We do need to know how many persons will be accompanying
you for the October 29th banquet. The ticket cost is $12.50
each. Your own ticket will be complimentary. For ticket
reservations, please write by Wednesday, October 25th to:

        Huron Area Chamber of Commerce
        15 Fouth Street S.W.
        Huron, South Dakota 57350
        or call, (605) 352-8775

    Again, we are proud of your accomplishments and
would like to recognize you at the awards banquet.

With Best Regards,

SPIRIT OF DAKOTA AWARD COMMISSION
Donna Christen & Marilyn Hoyt
Co-Chairwomen

Reminiscent Teacher Award
granted by
South Dakota Retired Teachers Association
to
Kathryn Larsen
In recognition of dedicated service to education and for preserving the history and for sharing personal teaching experience of the early years.
May 2, 2001
Date
Donald Kennedy
President

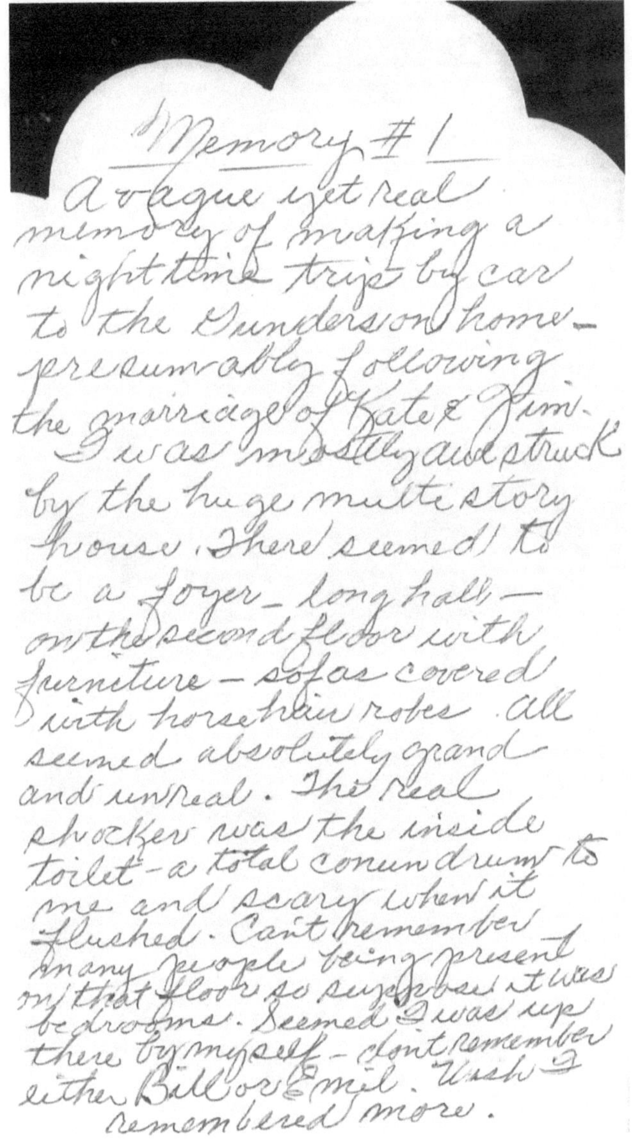

Memories of Kate's youngest sister Lena

Memory # 2

I can't imagine why Kate and Jim would have been so willing to have me stay over for days and back to transport me long distances after maybe a whole week.

I remember sleep walking and then later finding myself asleep on the floor in front of their bed. I must have been rather strange for them. I never got home sick and always felt important. I know I was a real chatter box and sometimes Kate would laugh and tell Jim I sounded just like mother.

I know Kate sensed I needed more attention but I think Jim must surely have considered me more than a nuisance.

Memories of Kate's youngest sister Lena

Sunday was definitely for church and definitely for putting on your

Sunday best clothes. I think Jim spent even more time than Kate grooming his appearance with the right neck tie etc.

If 20 guests were coming for later dinner that took place after church.

Surely Kate won the academy award for placing more food on the dinner table in a shorter time than anyone.

From Lena

Sunday 2/8/64

(1)

Dear Kate—
My dearest sister
This will be a long letter as it's been in my mind for at least 2 weeks. But imagine my surprise to receive your telephone call today. You are amazing and I pray in days to come you will feel amazing. [bodily]

Anyway — back to my letter which is how I am seeing your long wonderful life and of the vast influence you have had on several generations.

First of all your birth — the first girl following 3 rowdy boys and such a joy that your father names you after a song. And you never disappoint your dad in his intense desire that education is of great importance. Even though grade school was not the pleasantest experience due to ignorant people. That may have steeled you somewhat for the difficult entrance into Springfield where you felt lonely unprepared and attacked with all humiliating affliction. Did you give up? Did

A long letter from Lena to Kate

you quit? Never never never.
In that experience you had the
strong support of a loving proud
determined Father. (as u said
u could not disappoint him)
Now _ I can't imagine those
experiences at all as Lena was
definitely pampered comparatively
speaking.
Then you had the big sister
helper role, which took precedence
over your own preference of
time, money — opportunity.
In all these times you were
making unforgettable impressions
on persons you long since forgot.
Kate is strong! Kate is persistent!
Kate is remarkably faithful!
Kate is someone to be totally
trusted and respected.
Kate is as solid and strong
as that good name Kate.
Kate is courageous — Kate is
willing to push ahead and
bring others along with her.
(You and Katherine Hepburn)

Well — not strange at all that handsome Jim would take ② note of this vivacious redhead — This marvelous young woman somewhat daring but completely a lady with so much talent.

Ah yes — "My Jiminy, he found a wonderful wife!" Grandma Gunderson knew immediately and mother Wilson considered Jim more than a knight in shining armor. He was so special when she got "a feeling in her bones" that you would make a Sunday visit we had to kill the best chicken fryer and she made lemon pie — especially for Jim.

I remember what a blessing you were to visit Grandma Gunderson when she was in her old age in her little house. I'm sure your visit was the highlight of her week. And then there was Selmer — and all the rest.

Well the Salem Lutheran Church soon gave membership and baptism to one of their hardest working most dedicated members.

And how many years was that? And how many people? And how many young people and families blessed for the rest of their lives spiritually — musically — with lasting cherished memories.

And the farming —
and the gardening —
and the family dinners —
And the teaching — all of it happening at once being a wife, mother, teacher, friend, organizer, number 1 person expected to take charge.

Then you had your political chapter — the active one, and the county office. There again your high code of ethics and honesty came thru loud and clear I am sure. And you expanded your influence. And your own new impressions of government.

And of course that all trained you to be another kind of
Saleswoman.

Avon was probably one of ③
your least stressful adventures
and sort of fun in that you
again expanded your already
huge number of friends.
Until ___ you became the
First Lady of Jerauld County —
and Wessington Springs.
Almost Everyone knows Kate — the
special person named Kate.

Now — you are also a
common name in Buffalo
County and Brule — and
certainly so loved and so
missed by all your former
household, And the Larsen
family ___ large in number —
all so proud to think of you
as a step mother and a
grand mother — and a wife.
None can ever forget you as
your character is so strong
and stalwart — Yes that's
the word STALWART.

The family of Anna & Charles Wilson scattered all over the promised land, until the youngest generation have all been introduced and carry great memories of Kate.

So — how many lives have you impacted? It has to be many thousands, and you aren't through yet. Every doctor and nurse and helper has to be astounded at your courage and your example of ~~kin~~ patience and living Christian faith.

These words are not really adequate to include the special challenges and accomplishments of your life Kate, but they are a small sampling.

I am so proud to have you as a sister, and so happy for all your family to have as wonderful role model.

I know you were frustrated in not hearing my end of

40

the telephone conversation.
I was saying that both
of us are doing better than
average presently. For 2
months Arnold has been given
a weekly shot to improve
the red blood cell count —
(causing his anemia) and
it has definitely helped so
we are very encouraged.
Of course when he feels better
I feel better because I
wasn't so sure he would Regain
his strength and I realize
how alone I will be without him.
You have experienced that also.
I know I am much too
serious a person and tend
to worry — (or have concern)
when that is truly a waste
of energy. I have always
felt a bit lonely for lack of
family but old age brings it
to sharper focus.

We see Duane and Margaret every week at their place. They seldom come here. Of course we love going to "the country" and enjoy their cats and ducks.

Lately we have been participating a little more at church etc. We actually went to the Democratic Caucus yesterday — an interesting experience. I'm not too pleased with Kerry — or Dean — but who am I to know?

By now you are a bit tired of listening or reading this letter. As I said I've been thinking about you so much and your remarkable life and really wanted to share some of my sincere thoughts.

Love and Prayers
Lena

I remember how hard Kate worked at whatever the task giving 100% if not to get the most out of any endeavor — farming — gardening, canning, cooking, visiting — and above all keep the family together. Family reunions were at Kates house over and over — come one — come all. Those were the most special of special times. We each experienced the closeness of family. Others hosted reunions too which we

For the Lord is good;

his mercy is everlasting;

and his truth endureth to all generations.

PSALM 100:5

now miss so much. Time and distance changes everything.

www.ingramcontent.com/pod-product-compliance
Lightning Source LLC
Chambersburg PA
CBHW021350150726
47989CB00005B/2186